MOTHERHOOD IS MADNESS

MOTHERHOOD IS MADNESS

How to Break the Chains that Prevent Mothers from Being Truly Happy

Maureen F. Fitzgerald, PhD

Motherhood Is Madness:
How to Break the Chains that Prevent Mothers from Being Truly Happy

For information:
CenterPoint Media
www.CenterPointInc.com

LIBRARY AND ARCHIVES CANADA CATALOGUING IN PUBLICATION
Fitzgerald, Maureen F., author
Motherhood is madness : how to break the chains that prevent mothers from being happy / Maureen F. Fitzgerald.

Includes bibliographical references.
Issued in print and electronic formats.

ISBN 978-0-9939840-7-5 (paperback)
ISBN 978-1-9880720-7-4 (ebook)

1. Motherhood. 2. Mothers--Social conditions--21st century.
I. Title.

HQ759.F58 2016 306.874'3 C2015-905723-X
C2015-905724-8

Edited by: Katherine Coy and Catherine Leek
Layout and design: Maureen Cutajar, Go Published
Cover design: Christine Unterthiner, Pilot Brands
Cover photo: www.Phototobinphotography.com
Cover Image: Created by Nicolas Vicent, the Noun Project

Contents

Preface

My mother and father divorced when I was a teenager. I saw my mother, who had spent her entire life dedicated to raising five children, walk away with almost nothing. She had no resume, no real job skills and was at the age where it was not practical to return to college or university. She ended up working in a retail shop because that was the most she could hope for as an "older, unskilled woman." My father, on the other hand, still had his career, his networks and half the value of our family home.

My mother seemed to enjoy raising a big family (a 12 year span) and never asked for much thanks. She also seemed reasonably content with sacrificing her career and livelihood for us. As a strict Catholic she believed that her role as a mother and wife was to be a martyr to her family. At the young age of eighteen I thought this whole situation was grossly unfair. However, I never understood why it bothered me so much until I started writing this book.

When I first began conducting research for this book I came face to face with some very uncomfortable questions. I knew that by simply asking these questions I would make some mothers feel bad about their life decisions, but I had to ask. For example, why do so many mothers abandon their careers for their families? Why do so many mothers continue to do the bulk of the child care and house cleaning for no pay? Even with full-time jobs? And the most difficult question I faced was this: Why do mothers today choose to have children at all when they know that they will likely have to sacrifice their lives and may end up divorced and even destitute?

Motherhood Is Madness answers these questions and many more. What started as a few ideas slowly morphed into three books about the situation of women today and the many barriers that hold women back. I wrote one book on motherhood (this book); one on corporate barriers (*Lean Out*) and, one on societal barriers (*Occupy Women*).

These three books contain all of the information, research and advice that every mother needs to tell her daughter before she heads out into the world. They include all of the data and research that would have greatly helped me as I navigated my own life – when I decided to get married, when I chose my career as a lawyer, when I chose to get pregnant and most important, when I chose to quit practicing law so that I could raise our family.

By researching and writing this book, I have come to learn that motherhood is made difficult only because we as a society make it so. It does not need to be so hard on women nor does it need to tear families and relationships apart.

As you read *Motherhood Is Madness* you will begin to see how the institution of motherhood and our personal biases work together to maintain the status quo and hold women back, not only by husbands (who often accept their role in the system) but by our whole societal system. You will also learn (in the form of 15 strategies) how to dismantle this system and build a new model of motherhood that is good for mothers, their families and the whole world.

I would not have been able to write this book if not for the following authors and their books. They had a huge impact on my thinking.

- Leslie Bennetts, *The Feminine Mistake.*
- Susan Douglas and Meredith W. Michaels, *The Mommy Myth.*
- Sue Monk Kidd, *Dance of the Dissident Daughter.*
- Adrienne Rich, *Of Woman Born.*
- Judith Warner, *Perfect Madness.*

I would also like to thank all those who helped me write this book and gave me their feedback. In particular, Karin Mizgala, Sandra Herd, Monica Beauregard, Mary-Jean Payeur, Mary Pappajohn, Christine Dearing, Denise Withers, Jennifer Leslie, Christine Unterthiner, Susanne Doyle-Ingram, Darrell Tomkins, Catherine Leek and my husband Paul.

I hope that by sharing what I have learned through my research, women and men can work together to free mothers from the shackles of motherhood and couples can live much more balanced and loving lives. I imagine a future world where husbands and wives equally contribute to raising their children, working and participating at work, at home and in society.

I think that with better understanding of the institution of motherhood we can not only create flourishing families and loving relationships but we can make the world a better place to live.

Introduction

"To say there is a sinister plot against American women is both overblown and exactly right. Technically speaking there is no War on Moms, of course. There is no concerted effort to kill or maim women who have children. But if some sinister think tank had spent the last thirty years cooking up the ideal way to make American women miserable, it likely couldn't have served up more unpleasantness than women now encounter on a daily basis." ~ Sharon Lerner

Mothers today feel like they are going absolutely crazy. They are exhausted, underpaid and under-appreciated. They feel like slaves to their kids, to their home, to their husbands and often to their careers – just like their mothers did.

Corinne Maier's best-selling book, *No Kids*, describes how devastating child-rearing can be. From ruining sex lives and relationships to sucking up every spare moment attending kids' soccer games, it's no surprise that couples are struggling so much these days.

So what went wrong? Why is being a mother so difficult? Did the suffragists and feminists fail mothers?

Most people blame mothers for this state of affairs. We tell them they are simply taking on too much and trying to be supermoms. We point out that in their effort to please everyone, they often fail. We tell them that all they need to do is slow down, stop being perfectionists and work harder at finding work-life balance; stop micro-managing kids and take a break. And if this does not work we remind them that they brought all these struggles upon themselves and it's their own fault for choosing to have children. We tell them that wanting to have both a happy family and a meaningful career is crazy. And we say things like, "You can't have your cake and eat it too." We expect them to lie in the bed they made.

The research, however, paints another picture. As you will see in this book, mothers and their choices are not the real cause of all these difficulties. Indeed most mothers do not have the option to scale back. Indeed 70% of mothers work outside the home and still carry the bulk of the domestic chores and child-rearing.

At the root of all these so-called, "mother's problems" is a whole "institution of motherhood" that we have inherited that constrains mothers. The academic experts on this topic call this system several different names such as, "the institution of motherhood," "momism," the "MRS," "the sticky floor" or "the mommy trap. "

Motherhood Is Madness shines a light on the mommy trap and shifts the blame from mothers to a whole system, consisting of hundreds of barriers and biases that make it extraordinarily difficult to raise children today. This "sticky floor" is so deeply rooted in long-standing beliefs that we can barely see it. Yet in combination these factors systematically curtail mothers' choices in many different ways, limiting options to such a degree that women feel they have no choice at all.

Here you will learn that motherhood is truly madness, but need not be. By looking at the expectations and pressures that mothers face we can see why so many mothers feel trapped and unhappy. Motherhood, as we know it, is complete insanity and it must stop! In this book I do three things:

- I acknowledge the reality of mothers' lives and describe the very real circumstances and decisions mothers must make regarding family and career. I challenge the myth that all motherhood is blissful.

- I provide information and research that shows the many ways that our society holds mothers back – from inflexible workplaces to financial dependence on husbands. This helps women stop blaming themselves and understand better why they are so stressed out.

- I provide specific action steps so both men and women can begin to challenge our outdated model of motherhood and usher in a new one that not only supports mothers and gives them the status they deserve, but also values children and families.

I believe that when mothers (and fathers) learn the truth about what is really going on they will not only free themselves from the shackles of motherhood but will be more able to contribute to making the world better for their daughters and sons. After all, aren't our families the most important "possessions" in our lives and isn't motherhood the most important job in the world?

I also want to remind all mothers they are perfect just as they are and that they are probably doing enough. As a society we are treating you poorly and unfairly and you deserve so much more.

Quick Quiz for Busy Moms

This is a quiz to help you measure the impact of "the sticky floor" on your life. Please answer the following questions and then read the summary at the bottom.

To what extent do you:

1. Feel overwhelmed by the job of being a mother.
   Never, sometimes, often, always
2. Suffer from feelings of guilt for not doing enough.
   Never, sometimes, often, always
3. Feel you had to choose between career and family.
   Never, sometimes, often, always
4. Feel you are not feeding your children well enough.
   Never, sometimes, often, always
5. Feel you should be enjoying your children.
   Never, sometimes, often, always
6. Feel undervalued by your partner and kids.
   Never, sometimes, often, always
7. Feel you carry the bulk of the responsibility for the family.
   Never, sometimes, often, always
8. Feel you are responsible for most cleaning.
   Never, sometimes, often, always

9. Feel you do most of the child-rearing.
   Never, sometimes, often, always

10. Feel you are responsible for most meals.
    Never, sometimes, often, always

11. Feel you are responsible if your children fail.
    Never, sometimes, often, always

12. Feel if you don't do everything, no one else will.
    Never, sometimes, often, always

13. Feel that raising kids is hard work.
    Never, sometimes, often, always

14. Think you are not an ideal role model.
    Never, sometimes, often, always

15. Feel you would like more financial independence.
    Never, sometimes, often, always

16. Feel resentful if partner does not help out at home.
    Never, sometimes, often, always

17. Feel like you are often alone in your struggles.
    Never, sometimes, often, always

18. Feel you have to do everything to a high standard.
    Never, sometimes, often, always

19. Feel you would like to contribute more outside the home.
    Never, sometimes, often, always

20. Feel you don't have enough time for yourself.
    Never, sometimes, often, always

These questions measure the extent to which you are negatively impacted by "the sticky floor."

If you answered "Never" to most questions, you are probably doing fine as a mother. If you answered "Always" to many of the questions, you are likely struggling. This does not mean that you are necessarily disgruntled or angry; indeed you may be coping fairly well. However, by answering in the affirmative it does mean that you feel the strain and difficulties imposed on you by the institution of motherhood. *Motherhood Is Madness* not only explains why you feel this way but also what you can do to make your life better.

Part One

The Institution of Motherhood

Chapter 1

Admit that Motherhood Is Madness

"While many women today feel more liberated, society now demands that they become superwomen – that they find the inner resources as well as the time and energy to do everything perfectly. And this pressure is not just on women who have paying jobs or professions, but on homemakers as well." ~ Riane Eisler

Not too long ago I complained to my close friend Jennifer that I hated doing all the "no-brain-work" around the house while my husband got to travel the world and meet interesting people. Without hesitation she shot back, "So what were you thinking when you decided to be a mother?"

I can assure you that although I had given significant thought to having a family (I was 37 when I had my first child), I never envisioned myself as I am now – a seasoned lawyer with a number of university degrees – changing all the diapers, cleaning all the toilets and wondering how I got here.

Like many couples, my husband and I both have full-time careers. When we married I was practicing law Monday to Saturday from 8 a.m. to 6 p.m. My husband had similar hours. We cooked, cleaned and scheduled activities. We shared all expenses. We have always been very clear about contributing 50/50. Then we had children and everything fell apart. We quickly realized that if we were going to avoid divorce or insanity something had to give. But what?

Research shows that many mothers feel just like me – exhausted and unhappy. Many are trying to be supermom while managing careers and families 24/7. Both those with careers and those without feel overworked, unfulfilled and out of control. This is because, quite frankly, they are. Women with children work like slaves in their homes for no pay and little recognition and they do it to a level of perfectionism that is shocking. And they do it with a smile, at least in public.

Yet the prevailing mythology promoted in the media and in our culture is that domestic immersion is blissful and deeply rewarding. From magazine covers and advertisements to sitcoms, women are generally portrayed as completely ecstatic about getting pregnant and thrilled to be playing on the floor with baby for hours on end. Even diaper changing looks easy and fun. The message is clear: If mothers just do all these amazing things they will be both happy and fulfilled. And if they aren't happy, it's their own fault.

Indeed, most people will tell you that those women who chose to have children, and who may feel unfulfilled, simply brought it upon themselves. They insist these women should not be so surprised. Others blame the feminists who convinced women that they could have their cake and eat it too, when we all know that this is simply not possible. Others think it's time for women to go back to the way things were; go back home and accept that motherhood is fundamentally inconsistent with holding down a paying job.

But when you look at the research, the madness of motherhood is not due to women's choices but rather to our whole society's beliefs about what mothers can do and ought to do. As a society we have adopted quite strict and narrow assumptions stipulating who women, and particularly mothers, should be. Most significantly when women decide to marry and have children they are expected to take on the full responsibility of raising children. As a society we expect them to feed, clothe and nurture these children from birth to 18 years of age (or more). We convince them that they must do this work for free and sacrifice their lives and careers for their husbands and children.

As a result, if children and families do flourish, it is at the expense of mothers. And if women are unwilling to make the work sacrifice, and choose to have both a career and raise a family at the same time, we make their lives miserable. As a society we refuse to create work conditions or provide supports that might make their lives easier. And to make matters worse, we tell working mothers that they must be perfect in their rotating roles of mother, wife, daughter and career woman. This bundle of expectations and pressure is killing mothers slowly.

In academic circles this bundle of expectations and assumptions about mothers goes by several names, including "the institution of motherhood," "momism," "the sticky floor," "the mommy trap" and "the MRS." Unbeknownst to women, when they marry and bear children they automatically enter this legally, socially and economically constructed trap.

Authors Susan Douglas and Meredith Michaels remind us in their book, *The Mommy Myth*, that this is the same problem that our mothers faced. "It is important that we remind ourselves of the tyranny of the role of the MRS, because it was what feminists attacked as utterly oppressive, and because under the guise of the new momism, it has risen, phoenix-like, and burrowed its way once again into the media and into the hearts and minds of millions of mothers."

This mommy trap was best described in Betty Friedan's 1963 best-seller *The Feminine Mystique*. Like our mothers, women today across North America are still financially dependent on husbands, are told to choose between work and family and are carrying the bulk of both the child-rearing and the domestic chores. Mothers are still expected to be responsible for the well-being of their children (our future generation), the upkeep of the home, the maintenance of the marriage and the care of aging parents.

The Bottom Line. Although women, with the help of the suffragists and feminists, have made some legal and political strides, mothers have barely advanced in terms of status, power or freedom. Mothers today are pretty much in the same situation as our mothers were. We are often slaves to the home and our children and if we choose to work at a paying job, our lives become even more impossible. Although we like to blame women for their unhappiness and "poor" choices, research shows that when women marry they get caught in the "sticky floor" of motherhood. This sticky floor consists of hundreds of factors that systematically curtail women's choices. In essence, we constrict mothers' choices so severely that if they do choose to have a family, they suffer in ways that men simply do not.

What To Do. First of all, we must admit that life as a mother is difficult and that many mothers are exhausted and unhappy. As a result relationships and families suffer. Instead of blaming mothers we need to look at the many barriers that prevent mothers from living a full and balanced life – both working and raising children. We must identify and challenge all of the factors that make up the so-called "sticky floor," including our expectations and assumptions of mothers. We must stop telling women that they have made poor choices and acknowledge that the choices we give mothers are tightly constricted. In other words, we must observe like anthropologists the institution of motherhood and remove those hurdles that keep mothers trapped.

Chapter 2

Stop Asking Mothers to Choose Career or Family

"The fact that women have the intellectual capacity of rocket scientists, the biological capabilities of mothers, the learned and inherent talents of nurturers, and the socially imposed responsibilities of domestic managers, does not mean these pieces will fit neatly together at once." ~ Karen Engberg

I can't tell you how many times I have been told, "You can't have your cake and eat it too." For mothers today this message states very clearly: You cannot have children and a career, or at least not at the same time. It also implies you should not set your sights too high; you should not expect to have both financial success and domestic happiness – and you should give up trying.

As psychologist Selma Greenberg says, this is never a message aimed at men. "It was (and perhaps in some places still is) quite common for people to say to the woman who hires a substitute to care for her children, 'If you didn't want to raise them, you shouldn't have had them.' This kind of comment has never been directed to men."

Throughout my career as a lawyer and academic, I was told in no uncertain terms that I had to choose between job and family. Often it was done in the most kind-hearted manner by well intending colleagues who wanted to save me from a tortured life. Sometimes the words were spoken in a patronizing tone, "Go home and look after your children," or "Your children will grow up so fast!"

I was told I could either climb the corporate ladder or I could go home and look after children. In addition to this I was told I'd have to sacrifice my entire income, my career, my sense of meaning and my contributions to the larger world if I wanted to spend more time with the people I loved, including my husband, children, relatives and friends. Statements meant to placate me just added to my guilt about possibly making bad or selfish choices; all the while I just wanted to be a whole human being.

As a young lawyer I was told:

- You cannot reduce your work hours without facing a severe career setback like loss of seniority and credibility.
- Don't expect the same proportionate income or upward career mobility if you choose to work part time.
- If you want to be taken seriously as a lawyer you have to hire a full-time nanny and house keeper and rarely see your children.
- You will find it almost impossible to get back into the practice of law if you leave for any length of time and you'll need to start at the bottom if you do return.
- If you stop practicing law full time you will suffer large financial setbacks like loss of income, loss of seniority and loss of retirement savings.

Years ago I thought these comments made complete sense. I mean, if you don't work, of course you don't get paid or promoted. I told myself that this was just the way things were and I never thought to question that reality. I was a product of my socialization and had become convinced that the only way to earn good money was to do it in this particular way. I believed in Ayn Rand and her individualist market-economy theories. I believed that it would have been arrogant and selfish for me to ask anyone to accommodate me. Even my best friends told me things like, "It's a tough choice, Maureen, but it's still your choice!" or worse yet, "Maybe you should just go home if you can't stand the heat."

Indeed, when we make mothers choose all or none – between children or paid work – we cause women serious harm. This is described by Leslie Bennetts in her book *The Feminine Mistake* as a type of psychological castration because the "choices" women face are, quite simply, "unnatural." Excessive work severs a mother from her need to be physically present in caring for her child and excessive motherhood severs a mother not only from her ability to financially provide for her family but also from her sense of agency as a fully developing human. Author Judith Warner suggests that asking mothers to choose one or the other, "does violence to mothers, splitting them unnaturally, within themselves."

As I look back, I understand better why I could not get rid of the knot in my stomach that kept screaming, "It's not fair; why should my husband get to do it all, but not me? Is it really my choice?" At the same time, I felt like I was being split in two. Like a modern version of Meryl Streep's character in *Sophie's Choice* who, during the Holocaust, was forced to choose between her two children, I felt like I was in a straitjacket. It took me 7 years of reading and research to figure out why I felt this way and what was really going on.

Now I realize that our society simply expects mothers to bear the bulk of the burden and cost of child-rearing. We expect them to give up paid work or else keep a job but also carry the weight of children and home. It's not quite evil, it's just what we have come to accept as the status quo.

But what is evil is the distortion of this reality. We intentionally or unintentionally hide these facts from mothers because we don't want them to rebel. We use propaganda to hide this truth and convince mothers that this is somehow normal and natural. Then we tell mothers that if they don't like the way things are then they should make better choices. This is called "choice rhetoric" and is a very powerful tool at keeping mothers trapped. The following excerpt from my book *Lean Out* explains choice rhetoric:

> The "choice" we give mothers in our society today may appear *free* but it is extraordinarily narrowed by the options. In effect we place women between a rock and a hard place. Those women who want a family life and also a career are given this narrow choice: If they choose to have a family, they must sacrifice their family or their job. They cannot have both (like men can). If they want to have high-paying and demanding careers as executives or CEOs, they must hire someone else to care for their children because the work is not flexible. If they really want to raise a family, they cannot take on a job of any significant responsibility, influence or authority because it's mutually exclusive.

In her best-selling book, *Lean In,* Sheryl Sandberg describes a mother's choice this way:

> Women are surrounded by headlines and stories warning them that they cannot be committed to both their families and careers. They are told over and over again that they have to choose, because if they try to do too much, they'll be harried and unhappy. Framing the issue as "work-life balance" – as if the two were diametrically opposed – practically ensures work will lose out. Who would ever choose work over life?

In her book, *Perfect Madness*, Warner suggests that the choice that mothers make is not at all easy or natural. Mothers make decisions to work or stay home out of a very "immediate and pressing sense of personal necessity" that includes money, status, ambition, the needs of children and the needs of the family as a whole. Her long list includes the following:

- Husband's work schedules
- Availability of quality and inexpensive childcare
- Job flexibility
- School hours and school holidays

- Sick children
- Jobs that are joyless and low paying

Warner describes this beautifully. "And all of those aspects of personal necessity are part and parcel of the condition of motherhood – not external to it, not accessory to it, not a 'selfish' deviation from it." In other words, the paths of mothers are not so much "chosen" as "devolved" from the material conditions of their families and our society's requirements.

As Pamela Stone, Professor of Sociology at Hunter College, says, this "choice rhetoric" assumes that feminists have been successful and that women have wide discretion in what they do with work and family, when in reality women's choices rarely reflect their true preferences.

But the most insidious costs to forcing mothers to choose relates to her family relationships. Research shows that women who feel they have choices are happier and so are their families. Warner states that not just women, but also children and husbands are better off when women have real choices. In other words, when mothers are given the opportunity to work for pay *and* raise their children, everyone wins. This is because there is no inherent conflict between providing for our children and nurturing them; as fathers can attest – because they've been doing it for years – both are equally beneficial for children, the caregiver and the world.

In their book *Getting to 50/50*, Sharon Meers and Joanna Strober gathered extensive research on the benefit of having mothers at work and found that a mother's freedom to choose is very important. "There is no credible evidence that being in child care as opposed to staying home full time with a parent is harmful to children. There is evidence that if you stay home full time when you'd rather be working or if you work full time when you believe its harmful to your child, your unhappiness may affect how well you relate to your child. If you follow your own beliefs, you'll probably be a better parent." Finally, Professor Stephanie Coontz found that, "working wives report fewer feelings of distress than wives who stay home and they are more likely to believe that their marriages are egalitarian."

It shouldn't come as a surprise that when a woman can make her own decision about whether to be a lawyer, an accountant, a mail carrier or administrative assistant and a caregiver, or some combination, she will be happier. If she feels as though her ambitions are thwarted when she is caring for children, she will be unhappy.

But perhaps most important is the modern reality that most mothers do not even have the choice to work or not. They need money to support their families. In 1965 the percentage of women who worked out of the home was 33% and in 2000 that number was 71%. According to the 2011 United States Census Bureau statistics, mothers are the sole or primary income providers in a record of 40% of families with young children. The study also found that 65% of women with children were working outside the home in 2011, as compared with 37% in 1968 (*Revisiting Gender*, 2014).

The Bottom Line. We continue to tell women that they must choose between career and family. We tell them that they, not their husbands, must sacrifice career and income so that the next generation can be raised. How do we do this? By accepting absurd work hours as the norm, by weighing mothers down with all the domestic and social responsibilities and by failing to provide reasonably priced supports to allow mothers to work and raise a family at the same time. In essence, we create a world where mothers who stay home have no hope of a career and mothers who work for pay have no hope of having a family life. Sacrificing career and income is the expected price of producing children.

What To Do. We need to stop telling women they have to choose between career and family. We must accept the reality that most women work out of necessity and that women have both worked and raised families for centuries. We should not continue to expect mothers to sacrifice their family life for their work life or vice versa. Asking women to make this choice not only stunts women, but it stunts families and our advancement as human beings. We must stop making mothers feel guilty for their choices. It should be accepted as normal for mothers to want both a high-paying job and a happy family, just like fathers do.

As described by Catherine Dee: "Women's rights activists believe moms should have the flexibility both to do their jobs and to attend to needs at home; after all, working and raising America's next generation are both valuable pursuits. The majority of girls (60 percent in one survey) believe they'll need or want to take time off from a career to have children, and they should be able to easily do this without harming their career advancement."

Chapter 3

Don't Expect Women to be Unpaid Servants

"Did having a uterus really mean you loved scrubbing toilet bowls, and having a scrotum mean you couldn't even see dirt?" ~ Susan Douglas and Meredith Michaels

"When women shoulder a disproportionate share of responsibility for housework, their perceptions of fairness and marital satisfaction decline, and...marital conflict and women's depression increases." ~ Leslie Bennetts

Neither my husband nor I expected me to become an unpaid servant. He never expected me to do all the child-rearing as well as all the tedious and mundane housework. But I do, even with a full-time job. I make the lunches, I buy the groceries, I plan the meals, I organize weekend events, I arrange music lessons – and that's just the predictable stuff. I pick up the kids from school when they are sick, I drive them to dentist, doctor and eye appointments and I stay home from work on every Professional Activity (PA) day and holiday, which is about 45 days annually, not including summer holidays. When I worked for a corporation, I used up every single vacation day and then took unpaid days for the rest.

I get paid absolutely nothing for this work. In fact, corporations and governments penalize me by saying that this work is not only worthless for counting in our Gross Domestic Product (GDP) but is also so simple as to be irrelevant to the world of business and work. When I applied for a job after having children, one interviewer looked at my resume with distain, as if I had been doing nothing for 3 years. Since

I made little income during those years, I was not allowed to buy disability insurance in case I got sick. Nor was I able to add to my retirement savings. In essence, my work inside the home not only has no value, but is invisible and carries a stigma that can never be removed.

Research shows that when a woman marries, her contribution to housework increases by approximately 7 hours a week. Just by tying the knot! Whether we like to admit it or not, the housekeeping responsibilities remain solidly in the domain of women. In their book *The Career Mystique*, Phyllis Moen and Patricia Roehling found that when couples marry, not only does the amount of time a woman spends doing housework increase, but that a man's *decreases* by 33%.

And why is this so? Do women like doing this work? Are they naturally better at it? Research suggests otherwise and blames this imbalance squarely on the shoulders of our socialization and societal expectations. For women, this conditioning starts in childhood with us simply copying our mothers as role models. As Selma Greenberg, an expert in this area, suggests, "One of the most powerful ways mothers and fathers transmit to children their ideas on what kinds of adults they should grow up to be is through the parents' own behavior. By looking, listening, by observing children also learn a lot about their place, their station in life."

From a very young age, girls are programmed in ways that boys are not. This conditioning is reinforced on television, through the Internet and in advertising. We are fed a very specific and narrow definition of what it means to be a girl, a woman, a wife and a mother. For instance, Greenberg tells us, "They [parents] instruct girls and boys differently, they offer each different play materials and opportunities, but most important mothers and fathers model different behaviors, skills, attitudes and abilities."

Here is some research from my book, *Wake Up Sleeping Beauty*:

> Research shows that parents treat baby girls very differently than baby boys. Although we might notice it, we don't see the full extent of the differential treatment, understand why we do it or recognize the harm it causes.
>
> In my first year of university I learned about the astounding "pink diaper research." In this study, college researchers invited parents to come into a room and hold various babies, none of whom were their own children. Unbeknownst to the parents, babies were dressed in pink and blue diapers at random. Some baby boys were in pink diapers. Some baby girls were dressed in blue diapers. The researchers then observed the parents interacting with the babies.
>
> The results were remarkable. Those babies dressed in pink were typically held more carefully and described by the parents as fragile, sweet and cute. The babies dressed in blue were held more firmly and described by parents as sturdy, healthy, strong and alert.

As for domestic responsibilities, author Leslie Bennetts explains it this way, "In general, women have felt obliged to perform housework, and men have assumed that domestic work is primarily the responsibility of mothers, wives, daughters and low-paid female housekeepers. In contrast men's participation in housework has appeared optional." Because society expects females to do this work, they do it. Indeed they do it for no money, status or recognition.

Even if you have three university degrees, as a mother you are expected to clean toilets and wash floors. And if you choose to hire someone else to do this work you will be expected to hire, manage and fire that help. In addition you will be expected to take on home maintenance and upkeep. This includes buying furniture, repairing household items and being at home when the electrician or plumber is available, which always seems to be during regular work hours.

To make matters worse, this domestic work, although important, will often be out of a mother's control and will also be seen as easy to do. This contributes significantly to women's unhappiness, as described by Bennetts: "The association between doing household chores – what social scientists call low-schedule-control tasks like making dinner, which can't be postponed until next week – and unhappiness is so pronounced that even when women reduce their hours to part-time, they don't get any happier. In fact their marriages may even suffer, because women working part-time end up doing far more of the household chores." Hope Edelman reinforces this thinking in her essay, "The Myth of Co-Parenting," in Cathi Hanauer's collection *The Bitch in the House,* and lists the many significant yet mundane tasks that women do, including keeping the refrigerator stocked, filing income taxes and finding a reliable babysitter.

For mothers, however, the most unappreciated and invisible job of all is what I call the "domestic contractor." When women take on the full responsibility of the domestic realm, not only do they do their own share of work, but they also manage the contributions of the other family members. Bennetts describes it in this way: "After the kids arrive, women's disproportionate burdens are exacerbated by the additional job of masterminding the whole domestic enterprise. Ask your typical dad what size shoes his children wear and you're likely to draw a blank stare. Try asking him about his children's teachers and playmates."

This critical job involves overseeing the entire household, making sure each person knows what to do and ensuring that each person does the job in a competent and timely manner. Almost every mother I know has a running list of almost two pages of tasks and chores, half of which are not her own, but rather reminders for others! Accompanying this master role is the nasty job of enforcer because, alas, the domestic contractor's alias is "the one who nags." When jobs fail to get done, the mother suffers even more from the pushback. She may get called a "nag" and often makes the choice of doing others' chores herself rather than having to motivate them.

When women complain about all this, they are told they simply need to let a few things go or lower their standards. It's seen as their fault if they can't find a healthy balance.

So where are the husbands in all of this? Are males born lacking in domestic skills? Could we have raised a whole generation of men who are incompetent at housework? Are males lazier than females?

According to the research, it is none of these things. Men are quite able to contribute to the home but choose not to and this is due to three reasons. First, most males, even to this day, are not expected to contribute as fully as females to housework. As Bennetts points out in her book, it's a matter of perception. "[M]ost Americans think that the division of labor is fair when a wife does two-thirds and the husband does one-third. When he starts approaching half, they think it's unfair. To assume that men only need to do one-third when their wives are working just as many hours as they are is just absurd."

Second, most men raised in the last few generations have been told they must be the "bread winners" or the solo income earners of their family. Because of this they take that as their focus, so often do not consider it their responsibility to do domestic work.

Third, workplaces are notoriously structured in a way that works people so hard and for such long hours that they are frankly exhausted after work and simply do not have the time or energy left for their family responsibilities.

What we do not see are the long-term and deeper impacts. When mothers get little domestic support, substandard or untimely help, and significant pushback they suffer exponentially. Lurking below the surface is a sense of unfairness, a growing knot of frustration, a decrease in self-esteem and an attempt to gain back control.

Many mothers silently accept that they have no power to change things and begin to resent their husbands, their children and their lives. They become women they don't even recognize, as described by Bennetts: "Maintaining some semblance of equity in your marriage can force you to deploy all of those nasty tactics you swore you would never stoop to as a parent, but nonetheless found yourself using the minute you actually had a kid. Bribery and punishment work; so do yelling and complaining. Threats are also effective, as long as everyone knows you mean business. With husbands, tender banishments are particularly useful."

To appreciate how downtrodden many mothers feel, just take a step back and listen to their repeated pleas for help with chores that are not even theirs. The situation is made worse when requests are rebuffed or labelled as nit-picky. A friend recalled this story to me. While cleaning her bathrooms and fending off her two young children's requests for snacks, she asked her husband if he could take a look in the garage and sort through the mess of tools and sporting equipment. Her husband said he'd be happy to do this, but that it might work better if she took a quick look first and let him know what exactly needed to organized. This is just one example of the difficultly mothers face when family members either ping-pong the chore back to mother or make managing of the chore so difficult that she finds it easier to do it herself.

Meanwhile, studies show that relationships characterized by a more equal division of labor fare much better. Women who are in two-income marriages, where both parents share the domestic tasks, are less susceptible to depression and more likely to be sexually attracted to their husbands.

In their book *Getting to 50/50***,** Sharon Meers and Joanna Strober found many benefits to sharing domestic chores.

> If you look at the wealth of research, couples who share work and family life more evenly have three factors on their side. First, wives are less likely to see their husbands as slackers at home (less "you jerk" effect); instead, wives may find husbands as more appealing because they snuggle their kids (more "BabyBjorn" effect); third,

employed wives are statistically more likely be happy with themselves (more "self-confidence" effect).

Meers and Strober describe the research of Professor Neil Chethik who found that an equitable division of chores led to a better sex life. In 2006 he conducted a survey of almost 400 married men and discovered that men who did more chores at home fared better in the bedroom. In other words, the more satisfied a wife is with the division of household chores, the more satisfied a man is with his marital sex life. As well, when wives were happier with their husband's contribution, the frequency of sex was also higher. As they say, "For years, expert John Gottman had told husbands that dumping family chores on wives is an anti-aphrodisiac. Gottman and other couples therapists have identified household conflict as the toxin most likely to stunt married sex life."

As well, research suggests that if husbands do more housework the odds of getting divorced are lower. As Meers and Strober say: "Couples where the husbands did 50 percent of the housework and wives did 50 percent of the earning reduce their odds of divorce by 50 percent as compared with couples where the wife did all the housework and the husband earned all the money. That's dramatic."

As for the drop in income that we sometimes think comes along with more engaged parenting, Meers and Strober describe the research of economist Robert Drago at Pennsylvania University. He looked at the data on men's income levels and found that, "Many men fear that spending more time with kids will hurt their earning power. But the numbers don't support that either. ... The hourly pay of men who did half or more of the child care was not statistically different from men who said they did less."

Finally, Meers and Strober describe the research of psychologist Ross Parke and quote him as saying, "Fathering is good for men. It makes them more likely to contribute to the world. It improves their self-esteem, their sense of efficacy, and their moral range because with children you can be more emotionally vulnerable. We raise men to be tough and closed and many fathers report discovering emotions they didn't know they had." What sometimes gets overlooked is that many men want to spend more time with their children but feel constricted by workplaces and stigmas related to paternity leaves.

The good news? Attitudes seem to be shifting toward more sharing of domestic work. Research from Boston College in 2011 showed that more than 65% of fathers said that that men and women should contribute equally to childcare.

The Bottom Line. Research shows that women do the bulk of the domestic work even when they have careers. This is mostly because we have been socialized to believe that domestic work is women's work as is masterminding the whole domestic enterprise. We are raised to think that work such as cleaning toilets and washing floors is not male-appropriate, nor is it worthy of pay, status or recognition. In fact, it is deemed mindless and easy. However, partly because this work is low-control and mundane, it takes a toll on women. And although husbands generally agree that chores should be shared, and many are contributing more, women still carry most of the responsibility. Couples who do share equitably are generally happier and less likely to divorce.

What To Do. Domestic work must no longer be considered women's work or menial work. We can no longer automatically assume that females are meant to do all this work or that this work is not worthy of status, income and recognition. We must never suggest that women are "built" to do this work or that unlike males they somehow enjoy mundane, tedious and repetitive work. We must start raising our children so that both boys and girls contribute equally domestically – from washing bedding, to setting the dinner table and cooking meals. Regardless of work obligations, husbands need to take on their fair share, and in doing so become role models for their sons and their daughters – and the cycle is broken.

Chapter 4

Never Expect Mothers to be Martyrs to Kids

"Too many of us allow ourselves to be defined by motherhood and direct every ounce of energy into our children. This sounds noble on the surface but in fact it's doing no one – not ourselves, or our children – any good. Because when we lose ourselves in our mommy selves, we experience this loss as depression." ~ Judith Warner

The idea of equal parenting is a hot topic these days. We see images of husbands bouncing babies on their knees and dads coaching kids' soccer teams and pouring over homework with their children. We love the vision of sharing all the ups and downs of child-rearing, from changing diapers to giving dating advice.

In fact, most young women today think this is precisely what happens. They think that having children will not change their lives too dramatically. They think, as I did, that raising a family consists of taking a few months off from a career and perhaps hiring a nanny to help out when they go back to work.

Research shows, however, that regardless of how many hours a mother spends at work, she is still the person who is primarily responsible for raising children and that raising a child is a very demanding job. Mothers today do the bulk of childcare, even when they have full-time careers. They are the primary caregivers, responsible for feeding, clothing and nurturing their children.

Mothers are also typically the ones who use up all their holiday and sick days caring for children. They stay home from work on the PA days. If you think you have an equal parenting arrangement, ask yourself:

- Who attends the kids' school concerts?
- Who picks up the kids from school at 3 p.m.?
- Who takes the kids to dentist and doctor appointments?
- Who plans and attends the kids' playdates?
- Who researches and signs up for sports, music and extra-curricular activities?
- Who meets with teachers?
- Who buys the kids' clothes, shoes and supplies?
- Who volunteers for school fundraising events?

Why do mothers tend to do all this work? Are mothers more skilled, more interested or perhaps more caring? Do mothers look forward to the "arsenic" hours between 5 p.m. and 7 p.m. when tantrums are common? Do they welcome the wet beds at 3 a.m.? Would anyone? What's actually going on here?

A few years ago in her book, *No Kids!*, Corrine Maier blew the lid off the myth of blissful motherhood by describing the truth about parenting. It became an overnight international success simply by confirming what most parents knew but were afraid to say: childbirth is torture; parents lose their friends; parents lose their sex life and desire; children are expensive and kids destroy leisure time and freedom. Maier says straight out that having children does particular damage to the lives of women since it often prevents them from advancing their careers and being fully alive. She suggests that no sane woman would accept this type of life if she knew the facts.

It seems as though we expect mothers to be everything to their children – teachers, trainers, nutritionists, sports coaches, massage therapists and guidance counselors – with no parent training whatsoever. We expect mothers to tolerate smelly diapers, belligerence, temper tantrums and vomit with a smile. Mothers also do all this child-related work automatically, for no pay, little recognition and very little support. We blame mothers if their children do not behave perfectly and yet mothers rarely see this distribution of responsibilities as unfair or a sacrifice.

Why? Because as a society we have convinced women that this is the ways things are. This situation is not only normal but natural and thus should not be questioned. We start young with the script: We tell girls that raising children is not only their duty and responsibility as females, but their reason for living. It is a higher calling. We remind them regularly through thousands of subtle messages that even in difficult times, raising these little beings is so worth it that women should not expect any reward or recognition.

The Mommy Myth outlines the specific ways in which the media convinces mothers that they should love their lives and embrace the status quo. The most obvious message to mothers is that motherhood is wonderful and to question otherwise is blasphemy.

One place to find this insidious and hidden message is in children's books, which often portray mothers as endlessly devoted martyrs. One that slyly takes this idea to its outer limits, however, is the book, *The Giving Tree* by Shel Silverstein.

Silverstein, known for his subversive humor and unique take on the world, stirred up some controversy with this story. In it, a young boy grows up beside a large apple tree. The tree (which is female) gives the boy everything he asks for: her leaves, her fruit to eat, her bark and eventually her whole trunk. Ultimately she is carved into a canoe and dies. The final page has the boy (as an old man) sitting atop the stump of the tree. Although this book is a parable for the mother-child relationship, when taken literally it reinforces that idea that mothers are supposed to sacrifice themselves for their children, and in this case, their male children.

Sociologist Selma Greenberg describes this North American model of motherhood as the "service station model," where the mother gives and the child receives. As the child grows, the mother becomes less important and the child becomes more important. This passive giver is not only slowly depleted, but has no real meaning of her own. In this model we lose sight of the multi-faceted mother as a woman and the other contributions she makes, to relationships, the community and the world.

In fact, most parenting books inadvertently ascribe the role of mother to martyr by focusing almost exclusively on the needs of the child with only the rare mention of the needs of the mother. Most of us assume that the child is more important than the mother and the mother's needs are secondary to the child.

A real problem for many mothers within this model is that they become someone else and inadvertently lose themselves. Author Riane Eisler suggests that this pressure to be something that we are not causes us to disconnect from our real life experiences and ourselves. We become accustomed to believing outside messages and stop listening or believing the internal messages that ensure our safety, health and sanity.

The cost to mothers is described by Judith Warner:

> Too many are eaten up by resentment toward their husbands, who are not subjected to the same heartless pressure. Too many are becoming anxious and depressed because they are overwhelmed and disappointed. Too many are letting their lives be poisoned by guilt because their expectations can't be met and because there is an enormous cognitive dissonance between what they know to be right for themselves and what they're told is right for their children.

The Bottom Line. As a society we expect mothers to be martyrs to their children. We tell girls that birthing and raising children is their destiny, then reinforce this message through children's books, movies, television and magazines. We expect mothers to satisfy the bottomless needs of their growing children, we convince them that motherhood is blissful, that their needs are secondary and they should expect no recognition or reward. In essence we sell mothers the myth that martyrdom is the natural state of motherhood. We do not expect this of fathers.

What To Do. We need to notice the ways in which we burden mothers with child-rearing and notice what we expect them to give up when they choose to become mothers. We should look at the ways we expect moms to be martyrs and question the service-station model where mothers are depleted over time. Both fathers and our whole society must commit to taking on a significant portion of the responsibility for rearing all our children. It is important to recognize that children are not just for the benefit of parents but for the benefit of our whole society. They are our future.

Chapter 5

Recognize the Importance of Mothering

> "The feminist movement of the late twentieth century created a new United States in which women ran for president, fought for their country, argued before the Supreme Court, performed heart surgery, directed movies and flew into space. But it did not resolve the tension of trying to raise children and hold down a job at the same time...They had not remade the world the way the revolutionaries had hoped." ~ Gail Collins

Years ago my friend Karin invited me to play a little game. She asked me to take out a piece of paper and, at the top, write the names and occupations of those people who earned the *most* money in North America. At the bottom, I was to write the names or occupations of those who earned the *least* amount of money.

Predictably, at the top of my page were the names of Hollywood movie stars and professional athletes such as golfers and football players. At the bottom were occupations like retail clerks, cleaning ladies, seamstresses, teachers and mothers. What I first noticed was the number of women and female occupations at the bottom, but this was not my friend's main point.

She then asked me to turn the page upside down. What became obvious was that many of the occupations earning the most money were not the ones with the most valuable contributions to society. They were not the people you might want to accompany you if you were stranded on a desert island. They were not the most valuable to our communities or even leaders.

In essence, this exercise demonstrates that the way we value people, occupations and contributions in our society is drastically skewed. The social value of a person is often in an inverse relationship with their financial value. Like mothers, many other valuable workers are paid very little. Although we pay enormous lip service to mothers and lavish them with gifts on Mother's Day, mothers are clearly not seen as financially valuable in our society.

For the most part, the work of a mother is seen as not just easy and innate but also fulfilling and fun. First, we are told that this child-rearing stuff is actually very easy. In fact, for females, the knowledge and skills required apparently come quite naturally. We are told that nurturing and caring are innate for females, even though the research is far from conclusive. And to emphasize the low value we place on mothering, we as a society refuse to see mothering as an occupation or pay for it.

The message moms hear is this: Since mothering is so easy and natural, mothers should be able to do it all with ease in the most effective and efficient manner so as to be able to hold down a full-time job at the same time. The famous comment coming from fathers' lips is, "So, honey, what exactly do you do all day?" We take the work that mothers do completely for granted and make it so invisible that we assume most mothers are lying on couches, eating candies and watching sitcoms all day.

Every mother will attest to the fact that raising kids is a full-time job, 24 hours a day, 7 days a week. This job includes planning, shopping, feeding, cleaning, disciplining, teaching, coaching, mentoring, modelling, cuddling and hand-holding. It involves helping a child grow into a fully developed adult and a contributing citizen. This includes meeting basic physical needs such as food and exercise as well as the more complex developmental and psychological needs (did someone say puberty?). Advancing a child's physical, emotional, psychological, behavioral, spiritual and social development is no easy task.

When mothers are at home and have some task flexibility, the role of mothering often expands into school-related and community volunteer work. It can include driving children back and forth, taking care of other parents' children and caring for elders or neighbors. Indeed mothers tend to comprise the army of volunteers invisibly gluing together our education system and our communities.

Professor Selma Greenberg suggests that the idea of mothering being easy is a major source of women's oppression. She believes we have accepted the myth that the jobs traditionally reserved for women require little physical or mental strength and can be discharged without a sense of authority. We presume that women need less strength because they deal with the young, the old and the infirm. Men, on the other hand, are presumed to need significant strength because they work in the cold, cruel world doing things like working on assembly lines, filling prescriptions and reporting news. As Greenberg says, "Only when women enter the 'man's world' are they thought to need the qualities of personal strength that all males are assumed to require and the same dimension of authority as men."

As for mothering being innate, Dr. Greenberg debunks this myth: "Perhaps no notion is more wrong-headed than that which suggests the innateness of child-rearing abilities on women. ... So we leave young mothers to their 'intuition', offer them some simple and often simplistic advice from some friendly male experts – pediatricians, ministers, psychologists – and expect them to make it as parents." As a friend of mine said, maybe that's why we have so many delinquents. We believe that parenting comes naturally.

The other aspect of this myth suggests that mothering is fulfilling and fun; it will reap its own rewards. This suggests that if we are normal females, we will absolutely adore raising children and will find it intellectually, socially and emotionally fulfilling. We must recite the mantra: "Having children was the absolute best thing I have ever done. It is tough sometimes, but it brings me such joy!"

This of course is far from the truth. Professor Greenberg suggests it is both disheartening and depressing for mothers, who have loved and cared for children for up to 20 years, to realize that the love might not be reciprocated. As she says, "It is perhaps the most depressing truth about motherhood [but]...Once these realities are understood, mothers can take actions to achieve the measure of dignity, self-confidence, and ego strength necessary to enhance their own and their children's mental health."

The Bottom Line. Our society does not recognize the value of mothers or mothering. We convince mothers that mothering is easy, innate, fulfilling and fun. We expect mothers to work for no reward or recognition and do not consider mothering an occupation. We rarely admit that mothers do a massive amount of hard work both in their homes and in the community. We do not keep track of mothers' contributions so as to count it in our economic models that measure productivity. This complete devaluation makes the work of mothers so invisible that even mothers feel as though they are not truly contributing. Just ask any divorced mother who has had to explain to a court why she thinks she is as deserving of money as her ex-husband.

What To Do. We must dispel the myth that mothering is easy, comes naturally and is personally fulfilling for all women. We must learn how to value the complex role of mother and honor the work that mothers do. We must stop defining childrearing as "babysitting" and recognize it as a full-time job involving many skills and responsibilities. After all, the role of raising children is perhaps the most important job in the world and one that deserves both compensation and recognition. We must see mothering as a career or occupation and upgrade the status of stay-at-home moms and homemakers who are essentially invisible.

Part Two

The Cost of Children

Chapter 6

Make Childcare Available, Affordable and Acceptable

"Women are now the major breadwinners in a third of all American married-couple households, and the average working wife contributes more than a third of her family's income. But women remain much more likely to take time off from work when their children are sick, even when they earn more than their partners. Needless to say, one survey after another indicates that men also have more leisure time. Ask most working mothers what they do with their leisure time and you're lucky if they don't hit you." ~ Leslie Bennetts

I admit it. I placed both my daughters in nursery school from age 3 on. They loved it and my husband and I loved it. I, however, considered myself extraordinarily lucky to not only find childcare but also to be in a position to afford it. And yet, I still suffered the daily guilt and shame that comes with "giving up my children" to strangers and the sense that I was a bad mother. Every day I felt inadequate. I somehow felt that I should be able to both work as a lawyer and raise my children without having to resort to potentially "nasty nannies."

What I did not realize is that a fully evolved system exists that pressures women. First we make quality childcare extraordinarily rare and expensive, then we convince mothers that non-mothers (even fathers) are bad for children and that only mothers can properly raise children and must do so 24/7. We sell women the idea that childcare should only be used as a last resort.

In this day and age affordable and quality care is almost impossible to find. The only reason I was able to secure childcare was because I was attending university and qualified for the university's program. Even still, spots were few and the price was high. Most of my female lawyer colleagues, working outside the normal 9-to-5 grind, had to hire full-time nannies at about $20 an hour (after tax money) when they chose to stay at work. There is also the worry, at any level, of the quality of care being given, so we may overspend on childcare in hopes that the higher the amount, the better the quality. What makes it even harsher economically is the fact that our tax laws do not permit deductions for this expense even though childcare clearly enables many women to earn income.

Most public schools begin for children at age 4 or 5 – either in kindergarten or grade 1. As a result, parents who want or need to work for pay must cover the cost of full-day childcare for at least 4 years. For the next 6 years or so, these same parents have to pay for before and/or after school care since most schools dismiss at 3 p.m. while workdays typically end at 5 p.m. That's a lot of money!

This financial reality can be the breaking point for many families and is often the main reason many mothers who have careers choose to stay at home. It's purely economics. It's a hefty chunk of money to hire full-time childcare. Let me be absolutely clear. This lack of affordable day care is the main barrier keeping today's mothers out of the workforce and away from direct access to money.

This is why the topic of good and affordable childcare is so fundamental to the feminist movement, women's rights activists and forward-thinking politicians. Without childcare options, mothers remain slaves to their children and remain out of the workforce.

Think about it. If all parents were offered free childcare, they would be able to live lives that combine careers and family life. I suspect millions of parents would find amazing ways to not only contribute, but also to apply their skills and intelligence in ways that could enhance their own self-esteem and sense of contribution, as well as contribute to our economy.

At the end of the day, most mothers simply bite the bullet. Being either unable to afford or to rationalize expensive childcare, they often work at low paying part-time jobs to simply pay the bills and continue to do the same amount of work at home, stretching themselves ridiculously thin.

Reinforcing this financial pressure to stay at home is the constant media message that passing off our children to caregivers is not only shirking our responsibilities as mothers, but shameful. We convince mothers that stay-at-home-moms are the absolute best for children and that nannies and sitters are bad and even dangerous. Do you remember the 2012 story about a New York couple whose child died when under the care of their hired nanny? Of course you do. Do you remember the 1980s horror movie about the caller who psychologically tortures a babysitter by repeatedly phoning her and asking, "Have you checked the children?" If you are old enough, you may remember both of these. They feed the myth that it's dangerous to leave your children with anyone but a blood parent.

According to experts, this is just a symptom of a much bigger problem. Over the last 30 years, North Americans have slowly adopted a more problematic model of mothering called "intensive mothering." Professor Andrea O'Reilly coined this term in her book, *Mother Outlaws,* and describes the current ideology with its strict expectations of mothers. Unlike natural mothering, this model of motherhood is defined by our dominant patriarchal culture.

Within this model a mother's role is fairly limited. Mothers must provide 24/7 attention; the children's needs must be placed before the mother's; a mother can be totally fulfilled in this role; and mothers must lavish excessive energy on their children. O'Reilly suggests that this model builds upon the old version of the sacrificial mother, which denied mothers selfhood. It seems as though we continue to keep mothers so busy they have no time for selfhood.

Like the model described so beautifully by Adrienne Rich in her 1976 book, *Of Woman Born*, we still give women all the responsibility but no power. This casts mothers as the enforcers but never the creators of the rules. Mothers simply enforce the rules created by society.

Apparently the timing of this ideology may not be accidental. O'Reilly suggests that the model of powerless responsibility began to show up just as women were making strides in the 1960s and that the ideology is not only deliberately manufactured but also monitored. As O'Reilly writes, "It seems that just as women were making inroads and feeling confident, a new discourse of motherhood emerged which made two things inevitable: that women would forever feel inadequate as mothers and that work and motherhood would be forever seen as in conflict and incompatible."

This model of parenting flies in the face of research that clearly finds this type of mothering is not good for anyone – not children, not mothers, and not society. Children in high quality day cares flourish. Mothers who work for pay are less likely to divorce, are generally happier and have children who are well adjusted. According to sociologist Pamela Stone (quoted in Leslie Bennetts' book), "Since the 1940's, this has been researched every which way. People have always looked to working mothers as the cause of problems, but it always came out a wash. What's more important are other things, like the quality of child care."

In their book *Getting to 50/50,* Sharon Meers and Joanna Strober interviewed Aletha Huston, a University of Texas psychology professor and expert on this topic. She found that the amount of time that mothers spent with their children was not that important, but rather the quality of the interaction was. As she says, "Many people do not have the luxury of deciding to stay home full time, but if you do, you should make the decision about using child care based on your own beliefs about the costs and benefits for you, your family and your child as well as your judgment about the quality of the child care you can find. There is no credible evidence that being in child care as opposed to staying home full time with a parent is harmful to children."

Indeed research shows that working mothers and at-home mothers don't spend drastically different amounts of time interacting with their kids. Meers and Strober found that, "Non-employed moms do spend far more hours in the house with their children. But it turns out that working moms spend only 20 percent less time than their at-home peers in 'social interaction' with kids – playing games or reading books versus making dinner while kids run around the house."

Another obvious benefit of publicly funded day care is not just that we have more labor, but that we educate children better. According to Madeline Kunin, in her book *The New Feminist Agenda*, Nobel prize-winning, University of Chicago economist, James Heckman, made the argument that "one dollar invested in early education brings a return of seven dollars." Yet it seems that the American and Canadian public see education as a public issue but childcare as a private one.

The Bottom Line. Our society pressures moms to stay at home to care for children – 24/7. One of the ways we do this is by making childcare rare, expensive and socially unacceptable. Indeed, the economics of childcare alone or having to pay a nanny more than what you earn is the most significant way we convince mothers to give up their careers. In fact some modern stay-at-home mothers' mantra is, "Why pay a nanny more than I take home in pay?" Today affordable and high quality care is near impossible to find and to make matters worse, popular media convinces mothers that hiring nannies and caregivers is a shirking of their responsibilities and potentially harmful to children.

What To Do. Stop pressuring moms to say home with kids and question the model of 24/7 “intensive mothering.” At the same time make childcare available, affordable and acceptable so mothers can work if they choose to do so. This could involve corporate in-house day care centers or publicly subsidized care, like $10/day childcare. Other options include benefits, subsidies or tax deductions to reduce the full impact of the cost of childcare. We also need to combat media myths with research showing that high quality care is good for everyone and neither harmful nor dangerous.

Chapter 7

Question the 24/7 Work Culture and the Mommy Penalty

"If you've been raised thinking you can do everything, and your husband works eighty hours a week, and you work eighty hours a week, and he's not willing to budge an inch, and you never see your children, so you opt out – that's not really opting out; that's being pushed out." ~ Risman in Leslie Bennetts

Let's face it, we live in a rat race. Our entire society has fallen hook, line and sinker for the idea that the 24/7, fast paced, stressful work world is completely normal. We all think that the long work weeks, the 9-to-6 workday and working weekends is the best and only way for people (and corporations) to be productive. Although we all know it's not really very effective or efficient, we have somehow come to accept this absurd system of work without questioning its impact on human beings, and particularly mothers. It might work in the short term, but at what cost?

Workplace research shows that this type of work culture is neither good for our health nor our sanity. It is not good for our families and takes a huge toll on relationships. It has sucked the joy out of much of our lives to the point where many of us don't even know how to have fun anymore. We never relax, rarely play games or read for pleasure. We think that taking a break is laziness. This type of work life looks even worse than our parents' or grandparents' Protestant work ethic. At least they took weekends off! When combined with our current culture of compulsive consumerism, and intensive parenting, we rarely have a moment of sanity. This keeps us at the grindstone, producing and consuming, like mice on a treadmill working night and day.

Unfortunately, many of us have come to believe that in order to be really successful we must work this way. We also think that if we work part time we will have to take a disproportionate cut in pay and will lose access to good clients and high quality work.

Mothers who enter this 24/7 work world are rarely offered accommodations or adjustments to enable them to provide care as this may be viewed as discrimination. So rather than taking on a lighter or more balanced load, women, in an effort to prove themselves worthy, often take on even more. It is not uncommon for a successful professional woman to state that she has to work twice as hard to stay at par with her male peers. As a result, women and mothers work longer hours, take on more responsibilities and dare not make any mistakes. This is the price they are told they must pay if they wish to have a high paying and interesting job.

If we dare ask for reprieve (like maternity leave, flextime or part-time work) we may be told that wouldn't be fair to the owners or investors who are driven by profit or to other employees who do not have children. We are told that not only does it make bad economic sense to give us more choices, but that it is fundamentally unfair. We stagger back to our offices and beat ourselves up for even asking.

Yet the 24/7 work ethic has been called into question. In their book, *Getting to 50/50*, Sharon Meers and Joanna Strober review the research that shows that the 24/7 workplace is not as effective as we think. As they say, "Most bosses don't see the problem of pushing employees to the max because they get the results they want – short term, at least. The 24/7 ethic is a gross perversion of the good old-fashioned work ethic and its costs us a lot in productivity."

Meers and Strober also talk about how our modern work world has become tangled up with masculinity in an odd way. "How many moms do you know who boast about their long work hours? Too many men think that success requires that they prioritize work over family and in doing so they expect their families to accept their absences and continual use of their Blackberries." As they say, "What man would tell his kids, 'My job is more important than you?' Yet that's basically what 24/7 machismo requires."

Not only does the 24/7 culture hold women back, but so does bias or the so-called "mommy penalty." When professional women choose to have children they are treated very differently than men. The minute a woman announces her pregnancy she is treated differently. In some cases workloads dwindle, in others women are switched to short-term or low-profile work.

Everyone seems to forget you are a fully contributing worker who is simply taking time off to give birth to and care for a child and who would like to continue a career in some shape or form after a while – just like the father. This type of negative assumption happened even earlier for Julie, a friend of a friend. At her first day back at work after getting engaged she was startled by the senior director of her workplace making an announcement to a group of her co-workers that now that Julie was engaged her next step would be to get pregnant and leave the company. No man suffers the same judgment when he becomes a father.

Meers and Strober describe the so-called pregnancy bias as follows:

> A 1990 study of business students found a "plummet" in the performance evaluations of women managers when they became pregnant. Subjects reacted negatively toward a pregnant manager because they expected her to be "non-authoritarian, easy to negotiate with, gentle and neither intimidating nor aggressive, and nice." In others words, pregnant managers were expected to act docile and feminine and encountered pushback when they behaved in the assertive, directive ways required by their role as managers.

Researchers at Cornell University found that mothers are about 45% less likely to be hired than non-mothers who have the same resume, experience and qualifications. Mothers are offered significantly lower pay for the same position. A mother is judged as a lesser candidate compared to a childless woman.

Another bias hits hard when women try to return to work after having children. As Meers and Strober say: "In our survey of more than 1,100 women, we heard story after story of how women lost jobs they loved or saw them as radically altered when they became mothers. For some the shift happened immediately, for others after many productive years as a working mom."

Here is an excerpt from my book, *Lean Out:*

> One of the harshest stereotypes that professional women face is that of mother. The minute a woman announces her pregnancy, she is treated completely different by almost everyone. No man suffers the same judging when he becomes a father. The two main inaccurate assumptions are that mothers are frail and in need of special treatment and that mothers are devoted to their baby and thus no longer able to commit to work. Although women have been devoting their lives to their careers for decades, there continues to be a prejudice that assumes moms are less serious about their careers because of their domestic responsibilities.

In my book I mention the extensive research collected by Professor Joan C. Williams and Rachel Dempsey in their book: *What Women Want at Work,* or the so-called "maternal wall." Here are some of the types of biases they identified:

- Labelling women who get pregnant as mother rather than career women – leading to a questioning of a woman's competence and commitment.

- Remembering the specific instances when mothers deal with family matters (like attend emergencies), even years after the event.

- Seeing women's absences for family matters as a pattern as opposed to a fluke, as they do with men's absences.
- Assuming that absences from the office by women are for family matters as opposed to business matters.
- Expecting that pregnant women and mothers will act in a more caring and nurturing manner than men or non-mothers.
- Assuming the birth of a child for a man will mean increased commitment but for a woman decreased commitment.

As they say, "Good workers put their jobs first; good mothers put their children first," Employers often discriminate against mothers because they think that mothers should be at home with their children. As they say, "Mothers who demonstrate high levels of commitment to paid work violate prescriptive stereotypes about the appropriate place for women."

Most people I meet have no idea about the ways in which we judge mothers. In fact most people deny adamantly that they treat women differently. So in order to measure this hidden bias academics use a tool called the "Implicit Association Test" that detects hidden attitudes and assumptions. According to several researchers, including Curt Rice, mothers face not just real career barriers but also an implicit bias. Rice, for example, found that a man with children is four times more likely to be promoted to a full professor than a woman with children. Here is an excerpt from my book, *Lean Out,* that captures the impact of implicit bias:

> We all pre-judge women, whether we like to admit it or not. We make grand sweeping assumptions simply because they are female and then treat them differently on the basis of this bias. We assume that females are the weaker sex and are not very physically or emotionally strong. We think they are flighty and scattered, prone to irrational thoughts and overly sensitive. We squeeze them into outdated stereotypes and convince ourselves that they do not have the

> competence or commitment to be in high-level positions. If they are mothers they face blatant discrimination. And because these outdated beliefs are buried deep in our subconscious, we do not even realize they are playing out and holding women back as a result.

One bias that is common is the belief that mothers make bad workers. Yet Professor Nancy Rothbard found that these beliefs about women are wrong. She studied a sample of 790 employees at a large public university. "Her study found that when women had stress at home they were *more* engaged at work and (consistent with the research that multiple roles are good for people) that a good family life gives women more energy to be good workers." (in Meers and Strober)

In other words, it is not the so-called "second shift" or home life that impedes a mother's career. It is the fact of being a mom as such, the perception of motherhood in itself that disqualifies her from opportunities and promotions.

Sylvia Hewlett's 2007 book based on her studies, *Off Ramps and On Ramps*, found that 43% of women took time off; of those women, 93% said they left expecting to return to work, but only 74% did so, with only 40% returning full time. The study also identified a "child penalty" where women who took more than 2 years off lost 18% of their earning power and 37% after more than 3 years away. There is a real perception that women who stay at home are not working and lose their edge. They are also seen as less committed to their jobs and the assumption is that they will take more time off for kids.

To compound matters, workplaces are usually completely cut off from the real complexities of raising a family. How many bosses ask men and women to travel and work late? Could a parent spontaneously fly to New York or attend a late evening client dinner? How many employers ask their employees about the impact of extended work hours? Employers either turn a blind eye or assume there is "someone else" at home to look after domestic obligations. Many fathers are too ashamed to say something quite real like, "I will have to call my partner and see if she can cover for me."

When women quit in frustration they are told it's their fault for not being able to cut it. Maybe they are reminded that lots of women have made it to the top. So they are left with the thought that perhaps they did not work hard enough or strategically enough. Maybe they were not willing to hire a full-time nanny or talk their husbands into staying home with the kids.

The Bottom Line. The working world that we have accepted as normal is not at all normal or healthy. Not only are most workplaces family killers due to impossible pressures, but given the long hours, there is almost no time or energy left for family. Because we artificially separated our work from our non-working lives, we ignore the reality of family demands and responsibilities, as if they were somehow invisible. In addition, we discriminate against mothers by refusing to hire them, holding them back from promotions and expecting them to accept lower pay and less challenging work, simply because they can get pregnant. Indeed, these hidden biases and stereotypes are wreaking havoc on the career lives of mothers.

What To Do. We must challenge the 24/7 work model. We can no longer expect all workers to work such long hours, particularly under such absurd pressures. We must recognize that this model only benefits a few, namely corporate shareholders and senior partners, and prevents mothers from working and raising a family at the same time. It pushed mothers out of the workforce. If we really want mothers to be fully employed we must embrace the idea of flexible, shared and part-time work and these options should not be relegated to a ghetto or stigmatized. Those who hire and promote must be made conscious of their own biases. All corporations should have transparent hiring and promotion policies and a "return to work" policy for mothers returning from maternity leaves. There is no reason why we can't all have balanced lives – combining both work and family – but we can only do so if we fix our broken model of work.

Chapter 8

Ensure Mothers are Financially Independent

"Many feminists believe the role of full-time child-rearer is inherently oppressive because it is a role that prevents direct access to money. They might be right." ~ Selma Greenberg

"No matter how lovely their homes are, economic dependency is the proverbial elephant in the living room – the enormous issue that is almost universally ignored despite its power to destroy everything in its path." ~ Leslie Bennetts

The most eye-opening book on the subject of mothers and money is *The Feminine Mistake* by Leslie Bennetts. This extensively researched book describes how millions of women today get married, quit their jobs to care for kids, then end up divorced and destitute. By leaving the matters of earning income and finances to their husbands, women fall into the trap of financial dependency that wreaks havoc on most mothers.

Many women get married without fully understanding the consequences of their decision. They effectively enter into a legal contract with their husbands whereby the wives agree to bear and raise children in exchange for their husbands' financial support – for life. The wife often quits her job or works part time so she can take care of the children and the home. The husband often works full time and often earns most of the family income, which he shares with his family. Although this sounds great in theory, what many mothers do not see is the longer term cost of this decision. What seems like a logical decision about the children can come with a hefty price tag, with loss of career, power and identity a result.

When women quit their jobs they give up direct access to income. This means they have no salary, no bonus and no benefits. With no income, mothers aren't able to contribute to their personal savings and retirement funds. It also means that women don't typically have access to work-related life insurance or disability insurance (since they aren't working and there is no income to insure!). Although husbands are expected to share their salary with wives and ensure their life-long financial security, given the divorce rate hovers around 50%, this does not always happen.

Indeed, there is a commonly held belief that the income earned by the husband is his money. It belongs to him and thus it is his to share or not. This money is rarely thought of as belonging to the wife or the family. This is evidenced by mothers still seeking permission to buy basic things like groceries, not to mention personal effects. This lack of direct access to money, combined with the fact that most women take on the bulk of the domestic and childcare responsibilities for no pay, results in a master and servant-like relationship with their husbands. I find it odd that no one seems to care that women rarely have money of their own. I am sure men would suffer a huge dent in their self-esteem if they were required to ask their wives for pocket money each morning.

Of course upon divorce in North America (which happens in about 50% of marriages), this sharing of the spouse's income ends. The income earner (usually the man) may walk away quite angry that he has to continue doling out money to someone he doesn't even like, yet this is the agreement the couple entered into. Even the laws requiring alimony (court-ordered financial help to assist the lower-earning partner – usually the ex-wife – become self-sufficient) do not balance out the finances.

Research shows that upon divorce, women's standard of living drops on average 36%, while men's standard of living rises by 28%. Bennetts points out that single mothers have twice the bankruptcy rate of married couples. In recent years, alimony has become rarer and child support payments often are insufficient even to meet the children's needs, let alone the mother's. Recent research by Susan Solovic found that "only 15 percent of divorced women get any type of court-ordered spousal support, and then 5 percent of that number gets nothing. As for child support, it is usually inadequate and many divorced fathers don't bother paying it."

It's not just lack of money from divorce that is an issue. Mothers find it near impossible to find work that fits with child-rearing. Many workplaces are not inviting to those mothers who have been away for any amount of time. Mothers are accused of having no skills or knowledge relevant to the work world. This often forces mothers to re-invent themselves, start new careers or take jobs in lower positions, often for less pay.

The cost of becoming a full-time stay-at-home mom and leaving paid work is not just the loss of income and a job, but of an entire career. Mothers lose self-growth, the chance to hone their career skills and the potential to earn even more money as they move upwards in the workplace. Bennetts proposes that one of the biggest losses a woman encounters is the loss of earning potential or the long-term development in her as a valuable commodity in the work world.

She says, "Your own career is an investment you make in yourself, one that – unless it is interrupted or derailed – will pay dividends throughout your life. Some benefits are financial, some are intellectual or creative, and others involve different kinds of personal growth. If you devote your life to supporting your husband's career, all those dividends belong to him – as does the career itself. Ultimately it's his asset, not yours." Women are actually investing in their husbands' earning potentials instead of their own which, "makes about as much sense as putting a million dollars' worth of renovations into a house you don't even own."

When mothers search for paid work they face a world where most of the jobs are full time and where the part-time or flexible jobs pay significantly less, without benefits. After the kids are grown, mothers face even more barriers trying to get back into their careers.

Many women also lose their independent identity when they become mothers. They become dependent on their family for their sense of self: mother, wife, homemaker, daughter-in-law, etc. Some women eventually forget their own interests as they begin to identify with those of their husbands and children. As Bennetts says:

> In choosing the stay-at-home life style, they often don't differentiate between what they believe will benefit the family and what is best for them as individuals. Although the consequences can be horrendous, it's hardly surprising they continue to fall into the same trap. A steady flow of cultural propaganda encourages wives and mothers to think about their situations in precisely those terms – and to overlook their own unique vulnerability.

Mothers often feel that their decisions must be made for the greater good of the family and if she does otherwise she would be considered selfish. The loss of identity can be compounded by the value our culture places on mothers pleasing others and not putting themselves first. When taken to the extreme, this set of beliefs not only makes women financially dependent but emotionally and socially dependent as well.

The last hidden cost to mothers who give up careers to stay home is loss of power. In my mind, this is the most serious cost of all and is the main reason why mothers have not been able to break the chains of motherhood. We may all know a mother, whether a friend, colleague or relative, who is married and remains in an unhealthy or abusive relationship. But it isn't uncommon to simply shake our heads as if to say, "That's the way things go," as if there is nothing we can do. Yet, if you can look at it from a non-emotional perspective, the whole reason she is not leaving is that she has become powerless. If she has no money of her own and has children who need full-time care, her options are limited. If she left, she would have to find a high-paying, flexible job that would allow her to care for her children. Her decision is mired in economics.

As author Anita Roberts says, "Without financial independence, women cannot truly be free. For example if a woman cannot leave a relationship because she cannot support herself and her children, then she is trapped. In order to survive she must prostitute herself either within the relationship or outside the relationship as a way of supporting herself."

Solovic describes this situation beautifully:

> I have also sadly seen too many women trapped in unhappy and abusive relationships because of economic dependence. Women who have been full-time homemakers and have no marketable skills find themselves with no means to support themselves or their children should they decide to leave. So they bravely (or foolishly) look the other way when it comes to infidelity, they make their excuses for drunkenness, and they cover up the abuse. Eventually, their self-esteem slips away, and all that remains is a shell of a woman.

This power imbalance around money and earning capacity wreaks havoc on our relationships, our sex lives, our families and on our sense of self-control and self-worth. The ultimate irony surrounding mothers and money is that women are actually blamed for their financial predicament. They are told that they should have stayed at work and should not have let go of the financial reins in the marriage, another instance of the cultural push and pull to be both primary caregiver to the children and financial contributor.

As for taking the financial reins of the family's income, this is easier said than done. I have attended many financial planning seminars for women and have been told that I am completely wrong for not managing my husband's income or our family's money. I've also been blamed for not separating my money from my husband's and making my own investments – all good ideas. What many financial planners don't recognize is the psychological, personal and relationship side of money.

Often women delegate the responsibility to their husbands for many practical reasons. The husband may prefer to do the accounting or the wife may not enjoy the task. The husband may feel it's his responsibility, as the primary income earner, to do this work and may need that sense of authority, control and competence. To make matters more complex, some women come from a tradition where women were not allowed to have their own money or property. As a result many have ambivalence around money. Indeed, the whole topic of ambition and financial success can be problematic for women and girls. Mired in our cultural belief that females can count on males to support them, women were not taught about the critical importance of and skills related to financial independence – as a means to freedom and choice.

Having said this, all mothers must take full responsibility for their own financial well-being. As Solovic says, "Women make up three-fifths of all people living in poverty in the United States. The reality is that at some point, the majority of women in this country will find themselves solely responsible for their own financial security. That is why you need to start planning your financial future now, no matter what your current circumstances are."

The Bottom Line. When a woman marries and has children she may give up her career and become financially dependent on her husband. This comes at a huge cost to women and their families. Women lose income and the sense of security that provides. They lose not just jobs but entire careers and the investment in their own skills and experience that would provide later opportunities. They lose money, insurance and savings even if they leave for a short while. Mothers rarely get back to where they would have been had they not taken the time off. In effect, mothers are investing in their husbands' careers at the expense of their own. And should a women divorce she will likely be in a worse financial situation than her husband.

What To Do. To be truly free, women must have direct access to money. They must have economic power and financial security. This means income, savings and property. In situations where one person is not earning income, couples must have regular, frank and open financial discussions – both before and during marriage. Money that husbands earn is best shared at the point of earning to give the wife a sense that it belongs equally to her. All property, such as home and furniture should be held jointly and a wife should have her own bank account, although a joint bank account can be used to combine income for the benefit of the family. If a couple divorces it is critical that the cost of her giving up her job or career is compensated in some way (like alimony).

Chapter 9

Adopt a Partnership Model of the Family

> "Men are thought to be making their contribution to the children by doing just what some women want to do – engaging in paid employment in order to pay the baby's bills. While it seems obvious that working women are not mothering during the time they are away from home, why is it that fathers are assumed to be fulfilling their fathering role when they are at work? The reason is that the father role, like the husband's role, is totally undefined beyond its sexual and financial support aspects." ~ Selma Greenberg

I can't tell you how many times my friends have said to me. "Oh, Maureen, you are so lucky! Your husband is so wonderful!" Even when I explain that he really does only the bare minimum of the work required to operate our home, which is just as much his responsibility as mine, they still think he is a super-husband, just because he vacuums once a week and barbecues our family meals. No matter how you slice it, I have always done more, yet no one says, "Oh, Paul, you are so lucky to have Maureen!"

What this tells me is that compared to other men, my husband it doing much more. It also tells me that the standard for a husband's contribution to the family is strikingly low. But this is not all. It tells me that many couples have adopted our parents' "traditional" model of the family, whereby the main or only role of the father is to bring home "the bacon." It's enough that he be the breadwinner. I am embarrassed to say even my own family has begun to look like a traditional family – or as I like to call it – a mini-patriarchy. Paul goes out to work each day and I stay in my home office and write. We both work 9 to 10 hours a day, yet I do almost all the kid, dog and home-related stuff.

However, I had a light-bulb moment one day when my husband came home late from work. He had been late several times over the prior two weeks and had not called to let me know beforehand. On that day I caught myself yelling at him and threatening him that I would change the locks! At that precise moment I realized I had no real power. My threats felt like I was shaking a tiny twig at a ferocious dog. My strategies seemed useless and potentially dangerous. He could do whatever he wanted and my only option was to leave the family.

Somehow my husband had become the man at the top in a position of privilege and power and I had become the woman at the bottom. It was clear that he felt powerful and confident in his job and I felt powerless waiting for him to come home (while angrily folding laundry, of course). It occurred to me that if we faltered in any way and split up, I would be so much worse off. So how did we get here? Where did this model of "traditional" family come from and did it ever work?

Although almost all of us were raised in this type of family, many of us never noticed how power was distributed. In this system the father is typically the sole breadwinner. The rest of the family depends on him for food and shelter. This family is usually hierarchal, placing the father at the top as the most important and powerful person. He earns the household income and holds much of the authority over the money and decision-making. The mother does all the "family" and domestic work. In this type of patriarchal family, the father is seen as the head of the household and the mother is seen as support or secondary. In many families because of this inherent power imbalance, the father and mother relationship looks a bit like employer/employee or master/slave.

Many people believe that the "traditional" family structure works better than any other. Some people think this was a model designed by a higher power, with the male as leader and the female as submissive to the male. Many think it's best for society when men go out to work and women stay at home and do all the family work. Many believe that egalitarian marriages do not make sense and that women just don't realize how good they have it. Indeed, many of our current laws, social policies and religious doctrines support this model of the family. Very important are our taxation laws that allow couples to reduce their taxes when married or permit deductions from income for the costs of raising children.

What we do know is this: More often than not, this traditional model of the family holds women back. Professor Selma Greenberg declares, "It is this revolution that feminists seek and that reactionaries and conservatives fear. It is what leads antifeminists to assert that feminists threaten the structure of the family. They are quite right! Feminists have been working to break the unequal structures that have held both males and females enthralled not only in the family but also in the market place." In other words, any model of family that holds women back is not ideal.

One of the outcomes of this model is that women start to believe that they are secondary, as are their careers. In her study, "Fast-Track Women and the 'Choice' to Stay Home," sociology professor Pamela Stone discovered that even women who had high-powered, high-paying jobs implicitly accepted that their career was secondary to their husbands'. When deciding who would stay home, a father's preference to do so was considered, but more often than not, the couple decides in favor of the husband's career since his long-term earning potential is seen to be greater than hers. On a practical level, of course it makes sense to have the lower earner stop working. However, a flawed logic can result and women may become set on the idea that their husbands' work is thereby more important than theirs.

This type of family was described in the book *The Power of Partnership*, by Riane Eisler. She describes it as both a traditional model and a "dominance model." In a dominance model, the male typically believes he is more valuable and is responsible for leading, directing and telling other members of the family how to behave. He may think that control and strict obedience work best for effectiveness and efficiency. Eisler disagrees and recommends a "partnership model" in which all family members are equally important and connected and live in a type of partnership where members work together in harmony. Luckily, as suggested by Adrienne Rich in her brilliant book, *Of Woman Born,* this patriarchal, dominance-based system is neither inevitable nor sustainable.

A friend of mine recalls the first week at home with her newborn son. "It was the most difficult thing I'd ever done and my husband at the time had taken time off to be with us. However, midway through that first week, he suddenly made plans to go out for a work-related lunch. I realized with a lurch that this could become our new normal. He could come and go as he pleased – without having to make any arrangements for this new tiny soul in our lives – and I, well, I was going to be occupied. Fully. In the house. We were well overdue for an honest discussion of expectations; something I'd naively assumed was going to take care of itself. Our famously equal partnership was headed for some choppy waters."

Some suggest that traditional families are less likely to end in divorce, yet the research does not support this. Leslie Bennetts writes that in 1998 sociologist Hiromi Ono found that a woman is more likely to divorce if she has no earnings, but also that women who have no money or authority tend to stay in unhealthy marriages longer before divorce. This wreaks havoc on themselves and their families.

The traditional family also holds men back in one significant way – in his relationship to his children. Recent research suggests that the father-child relationship is very important to families. Apparently an engaged father is not only happier but so too are his children. In their book, *Getting to 50/50*, Sharon Meers and Joanna Strober describe the benefits to fathers of parenting. "In our first chapter we talked about what kids win from active dads. But it turns out that fathers need their kids – for health and long-term success – as much as children need their dads. A study conducted by the National Institute of Mental Health confirms that a man's experience as a parent, not as an employee, is the strongest predictor of whether he would have stress-related physical problems."

But they also describe how fathers are penalized when they decide to care for children – a so-called paternity penalty.

> A 2003 study reported that men who took even a short time off due to family conflict were given lower recommendations for rewards and poorer overall performance ratings. Meanwhile according to a 2007 study, if a father does not send signals to his boss or colleagues that he has care giving responsibilities, having children actually helps his career. He is given a higher starting salary than a childless man and is held to lower performance and punctuality standards.

It seems that men who take on childcare tasks are seen to be insufficiently masculine and are looked upon with suspicion. As they say. "They were seen to be bad workers precisely because they were thought to have traits traditionally viewed as feminine: being weak, insecure, emotional or naive. In other words the flexibility stigma is a femininity stigma."

The good news may well be that the traditional family is crumbling. Most families today do not have a sole breadwinner and stay-at-home mom team. In fact, the variety of family structures is endless. Single-parent families are as common as two-parent families and intergenerational families are also common. However, as Bennetts writes, "Conservatives also like to portray non-traditional families as a freakish anomaly confined to a handful of radical feminists and wimpy men – an impression that belies the facts."

As well research shows that women's autonomy is a real benefit to the family: "When women acknowledge the pleasures of having their own independence, right-wing conservatives often blast them for being selfish in seeking their own gratification instead of dedicating themselves exclusively to the family. Despite the reactionary claim that women's autonomy threatens the family unit, however, research suggests that it may actually strengthen the marital relationship."

The Bottom Line. Many of us live within a traditional family model, where mothers are responsible for child-rearing and homemaking and fathers are responsible for earning income. Whether dual income or single-parent families, this model tends to look like a "dominance-model" where fathers are seen as most important and at the top. This model of the family is often hierarchal and thus maintains inequality, keeping many fathers out of the household and mothers overworked and without control, autonomy or authority, often viewing themselves as secondary. This model is fracturing as we come to realize the value of independent mothers and the importance of father-child relationships.

What To Do. We must re-examine the traditional model of the family, primarily because the "sole breadwinner" and the "sole caregiver" rarely exists today. Indeed only 30% of American families fit this definition. There are many permutations and combinations of families and roles and we should be open to embracing them all. We must normalize the idea of the working mother and find ways to ensure that both partners contribute equally creating a more partnership type of relationship. We should stop trying to fit every family into the "traditional" mold that no longer suits.

Chapter 10

Value Mothers, Children and Families

"In this respect, mothers have not been unlike serfs or peasants. For serfs and peasants too were once viewed appropriately spent in service to others, to their betters." ~ Selma Greenberg

"Women today mother the way they do in part because they are psychologically conditioned to do so. But they also do it because, to a large extent they have to. Because they are unsupported, because their children are not taken care of, in any meaningful way, by society at large. Because there is no widespread feeling of any responsibility – for children, for families, for anyone really – and so they must take everything onto themselves. And because they can't humanly take everything onto themselves, they simply go nuts." ~ Judith Warner

Although we don't really respect the role of mothers these days, it wasn't always this way. Being a mother was once a full-time occupation. Although unpaid, the role garnered some respect because it was seen as critical to enable half of the population to work in industry (while women worked on the farm). The role of parents was seen as vital for raising and educating our next generation. Fathers financially supported their families for their entire lives and mothers, children and families were seen to be the bedrock of society.

Today, however, we have adopted an economic model that does not see mothers, children or families as valuable or as a benefit to our society as a whole. In effect, we allow families to flourish or fail without any sense of obligation to our neighbors or to the families in our community. This model causes all sorts of problems. It places a huge burden on parents, it causes single parents to slip into poverty and it harms children.

Although we see children as our future, under our current market-based ideology we tell ourselves that since having children is a "personal choice" parents should be willing to cover their cost. It's as if children are luxury items and, like widgets, we produce them for the benefit of parents. Following this line of thought, those who choose not to have children do not benefit, so therefore should not have to "pay for children."

As a teenager I was an Ayn Rand junkie. I read her books including *Atlas Shrugged* and *The Fountainhead* several times. I loved her black and white characters. I loved the idea that each individual could conquer the world and reach their dreams unfettered by evil governments and power-hungry unions. I believed in the power of pure capitalism, aggressive competition and the individual as hero. I believed in survival of the fittest. I loved it when the brilliant, workaholic, solo lead character won the game. I despised the losers who were lazy, good-for-nothings and I did not care what happened to them. I am deeply embarrassed to say that I never thought about mothers. I never wondered how they would be able to both earn an income and raise children at the same time. I also saw governments as "bad guys" who were stealing my hard-earned money and giving it to people who did not deserve it. This was my childhood brainwashing and I am glad to say I have evolved.

Still, our North American economic model is based on the thinking of Ayn Rand. Our current model places individual self-interest and survival of the fittest at the center. In this model, we assume that individuals can thrive on their own and we do not think that our whole society (through government) should help unless people are desperate. We allow industry to run its course and hope it will provide enough employment so as to keep people from starving. We assume that the profit motive and individual self-interest will drive everything and that supply and demand will sort everything else out.

Although this sounds good in theory, every government knows that this pure market model will not work in all circumstances. Because of this, every advanced society allocates public funding for people who cannot hold down a job or care for themselves. All governments also fund "public services" and use various tools to stimulate industry. There is no one perfect or pure model; governments in all economic systems play a critical role in assisting societies, not just to ward off starvation and prevent crimes, but to flourish.

Yet today, the motto directed at families seems to be, "It's not the government's responsibility to take care of someone else's kids." In relation to mothers, modern governments have been mostly negligent. The safety net for women facing violence and poverty is crumbling. Women's shelters are increasingly funded by private donations. Recent research by the Canadian Women's Foundation found that 21% of single mothers in Canada are raising their children in poverty. In Canada, 80% of all single-parent families are headed by women, or about one million families. Single moms have a net worth of only about $17,000, while single dads have about $80,000. In the United States almost 50% of the children are undernourished or obese and the US ranks at the bottom of developing countries in terms of health, poverty and homelessness. As the Occupy Wall Street movement indicated, our economic model results in the extreme rich and the extreme poor.

Yet the truth is that children cost a fortune to raise and rarely do parents get a large return on their investment. Indeed many parents find it difficult to simply cover the costs of raising children and they have less time to raise them. Because many couples need two incomes, single parents can easily sink into poverty, causing entire families to flounder.

The fact that children are not getting their basic needs met is reflected in statistics relating to drug use, poverty and crime. So why don't governments help mothers and families? Our current economic model simply does not see children as an important investment. Although we understand the value of investing billions of dollars in roads, bridges and armies, we somehow don't see the long-term benefit of children or their mothers.

The role of governments in this model tends to be limited to helping only those in dire straits and only to a minimum level. This has resulted in huge numbers of mothers in poverty as they struggle to work for pay and to raise children at the same time. Children's needs are not being met, impacting society via increases in delinquency and crime. By providing the thinnest of safety nets for mothers and minimal maternal supports, governments turn a blind eye to the link between the success of mothers and the reduction of poverty, crime, homelessness and the health and success of our whole society.

The Bottom Line. Our economic model does not really value mothers, children or families. It places enormous emphasis on individuals and self-determination. Children are seen to be the possession of parents and raised for the benefit of parents, not society. As a result, most governments shift the bulk of the cost of raising children onto parents. This forces parents to work long hours and spend less time with their family. Mothers may have to work several jobs or stay at home while their partners work long hours, all the while shouldering the task of childcare and home making. By not providing the necessary supports to mothers, our whole society suffers longer term problems such as illness, poverty and crime.

What To Do. We must recognize the impact of our economic model on mothers, particularly single mothers. We need to question the ideology of pure capitalism espoused by Ayn Rand and we need to work towards creating a system that does not harm children, mothers or families. We can no longer expect parents to carry the full weight of raising the next generation and must value parents, children and families. We must re-allocate resources so that poverty and other negative impacts can be reduced. We can adjust our strict market to ensure that everyone is taken care of. This might be a big shift in thinking for those who have been raised in our strongly capitalistic society, where we learn to be selfish and not care about the needs of others. But it is not only the right thing to do but an investment in our futures. We must remember that we all came to our wealth from the resources and efforts of forefathers and mothers.

Part Three

The Future for Mothers

Chapter 11

Compensate and Invest in Mothers

"Why should men be the only wage earners in a family, with the women utterly dependant on them for everything, having no money of her own? Since housewives put in something like ninety-hour work weeks, shouldn't they get some kind of compensation? Feminists offered answers that today seem, by turns, fantastical, utopian, defiant, and right on." ~ Susan Douglas and Meredith Michaels

Have you ever wondered why taxpayers pay billions of tax dollars annually for armies that rarely go to war yet we do not pay day care workers or nannies – or mothers? This simply means that as a society we value protecting ourselves from war more than investing in the people who are raising the next generation.

We pay fire fighters, police officers and garbage collectors from our public funds, deeming these services critical to society. We pay these people from our taxes not just because we value them but also because we don't trust our supply-and-demand-based market system to create and maintain these services. They are so important to our health, safety and prosperity that we dare not leave them to chance.

Not so with mothering. The truth is that although we see this role as critical to society, we as a culture choose not to pay for mothering or invest in families because we think that leaving it to chance or to the free market will work out just fine. In effect we have agreed as a society that we do not need to pay or support women for the work they do in their homes because they do it for free. Our actions suggest that we are just fine with parents, and mostly women, working long and difficult hours just to earn an income and raise a family.

Mothers are not repaid for out-of-pocket expenses nor are they reimbursed for the loss of income and career mobility that they sacrificed while raising children. Although some governments provide tax breaks to parents, these are barely enough to cover the cost of raising a child from birth to age 18. Indeed, not all parents can deduct the cost of childcare or babysitters from their income even though we know that in some cases, this is a kind of business expense since it permits parents to work. We assume that parents have enough money, time and interest to feed, clothe, nurture and educate their children without any help from us. So if children are not educated properly, grow ill or turn into criminals, society will solve that problem later.

In my opinion, if mothers faced the truth about how they are being taken for granted, they would all go on strike, immediately. Wouldn't that be something? Women could refuse to bear children until the rest of society helped them in some way. Think it won't work? There are actually successful precedents for this! How about the sex strike held by woman villagers in the Philippines in 2011 that protested an unsafe road between two villages? Within a few weeks, the road was safe enough to travel. Or the 2006 10-day sex strike by some Columbian women, protesting gang violence between their partners. The town where that occurred had the country's steepest drop in violence – a whopping 26.5% by 2010. Sounds like they might be on to something.

As for investing in women and children as a way to advance our society, there has been barely any attention paid. On rare occasions research is conducted by women's groups indicating that women could have a massive impact on the economy, but so far this research lies dormant. As for mothers who want to work, the talk of national childcare is rarely even raised and as a result women today are seriously under-employed.

Today, however, the family is shrinking and mothers are waking up to the cost of motherhood. The number of children per family has dropped exponentially. Many women simply decide to have only two children while others, not wanting the hassle and the limits on their freedoms decide against motherhood. Research shows that more women than ever are choosing to be child-free.

Demographers and sociologists have anticipated for years a rise in the phenomena of the child-free choice. Perhaps these women will no longer be condemned by our society as unfeminine and selfish. As Elisabeth Badinter suggests in her book, *The Conflict*, "Because more educated women have greater economic opportunities and more alternative sources of self-esteem than less-educated women, the rational choice perspective suggests that level of education will be inversely related to the importance of motherhood."

So why don't governments invest in mothers? Because governments make decisions without much input from mothers or women in general. Governments do not pay any attention to mothers, do not count their work in the GDP, only minimally support mothers and choose not to invest in mothers simply because they choose not to. Although they see helping mothers as having a positive impact on our society and economy they also enjoy the benefit of these "free" services.

Perhaps it's less of a conspiracy and more of a reliance on mothers' ignorance. So long as mothers do not demand these changes, governments are unlikely to help mothers. Until research proves that employing mothers will result in a massively better society or increase in industry (and taxes) things are not likely to change. As long as mothers stay silent, the status quo will remain.

If society truly valued mothers it would not simply provide emergency-only social and employment programs. It would see mothers and their offspring as an investment in its future. It would make decisions, laws and policies that not only support mothers in a positive way, but allow them to contribute fully and in doing so improve its economies, its communities and the world.

This is what I think: If mothers were in charge, we would not only value mothers, but we would probably pay them, give them holidays and provide them with retirement income. We would treat them like public servants whose services are invaluable to our society. We would reimburse them for all the out-of-pocket expenses needed to raise "our" children. This would include the cost of nannies and tutors as well as food and clothing. If they chose to have a career as well as raise children, we would allow them to deduct child-care expenses from their income. Although this might sound odd at first blush, we do this for other occupations.

We could easily introduce laws and policies that would not only keep mothers out of poverty, but also keep their children healthy and safe, ease the burden of raising children and free women to enter the workplace. This in turn would improve the labor force, stimulate industry and improve communities. But all of this requires an understanding about how governments make decisions, how these decisions either propel or limit mothers, how to engage in the law-making process and convince governments that mothers matter. Mothers also need to know how our laws discriminate against women, how aspects of the tax system are unfair to mothers, how they prevent mothers from being financially independent, and why governments choose to not fund programs that might help with these issues. Most importantly, however, mothers rarely know much power they possess together to influence governments' decisions and actions in ways that might better support them or at least stop harming them.

As Badinter says, "No country can afford to ignore changes in its birthrate. In the long term a nation's pension payments, power and very survival are at stake. To curb the decline in recent decades some European governments have re-evaluated their family policies." Without the benefit of a generation to comprise our workers and taxpayers, we have no industry. By not seeing our children as investments and communal assets, we are stunting our own growth as a society.

The Bottom Line. As a society we do not fully value the role of mothers. We do not see mothering as an occupation, we do not provide any compensation to mothers, nor do we reimburse mothers for out-of-pocket expenses or the cost of sacrificing a career and career mobility while raising children. We expect mothers to raise children out of the goodness of their hearts and take on the burden without many kudos or much support from the rest of society. Most laws and government policies reflect this attitude by providing only minimal family supports and few tax reliefs. All of this pressure can cause enormous financial and psychological strain on mothers. As a result many ultimately choose to have fewer children.

What To Do. As a society, we need to see mothers as critical to our society, both as caregivers and workers. We must pay them what they are worth and at the minimum compensate them for the costs of raising "our" children. Any support we give mothers not only makes their lives saner, but improves the lives of children who will grow up and join our society as citizens, workers and taxpayers. We must no longer assume that the free market will make this happen and we must ask governments to play a bigger role in investing in mothers.

Chapter 12

Challenge Laws that Hold Women Back

"Our reluctance, or outright refusal, to enact policies that would bridge the gap between family and work has contributed to disturbing national statistics: alarmingly high child poverty rates, declining college graduation rates and test scores and a growing chasm between the rich, the middle class and the poor. Our inability – for political, economic or cultural reasons – to invest in families leaves us vulnerable to being reduced to second-rate status in the global economy." ~ Madeline Kunin

As a lawyer, I am embarrassed by our laws, our legal system and our law-making system. Although our laws are designed to support us, the truth is that they are so numerous and so complicated that we have no idea how they work, in particular tax laws (which typically run in the thousands of pages). Not only that, the process of changing these laws is so complex and politically difficult most people don't have the education, interest, time or money to change laws that could actually make their lives better.

In her book, *The Price of Motherhood*, Ann Crittenden shows the various ways in which women in the United States suffer from what she calls a huge "mommy tax" or the loss of income that results simply when women have children. According to her research and the calculations of Shirley Burggraf, for a husband and wife who have no children and both earn $55,000, if the wife stays home to care for her child they lose $1.35 million in reduced income over their 45-year working life.

As for mothers, the biggest barrier to freedom is the lack of publicly funded, high quality day care and education. Through our taxes we all pay for basic education, from kindergarten to grade 12. Indeed public education is often referred to as the bedrock of advanced societies. This is because governments think that education is an investment that results in a high return – an educated labor force. However, there are fundamental flaws. Our public education is often insufficient and underfunded. Much of the cost of education is slowly being shifted to parents through the creation of private schools, out-of-school programs and tutors. School days are shorter than the regular 9-to-5 workday, so often parents are left to arrange before and after school care. Unlike prior generations, we now expect parents to carry more of the burden of educating this next generation.

Other laws that discriminate against mothers are very subtle. For example, divorce laws. Have you ever wondered why single mothers are so much worse off than single fathers? We know statistically that millions of single-mother families live well below the poverty line and it's not because they negotiated poorly for alimony or child support. In divorce, many mothers face a double whammy. They often get minimal alimony from their exes and, even then, some fathers may refuse to pay. Although some laws allow for the garnishment of wages of fathers who have fallen behind on child support payments, it is very difficult to go after alimony payments. And if the father is working under the table, his wages cannot be garnished, even for child support payments. Second, mothers who are caring for their children often work part time or reduced hours so they cannot earn as much as fathers who are working full time.

It is also assumed, quite erroneously, that divorced mothers will be able to quickly secure a job and be able to contribute financially to the family to the same extent as her ex-husband. As we know, however, mothers who leave work lose skills, seniority and opportunity and face discrimination in hiring and wages that can result in them rarely being able to earn what their husbands do. As well, we tend not to provide public funding for the poorest of women in divorce cases; they cannot fight for the support or custody that is allowed to them under the law.

In Canada, one type of law that crushes the voices of women is both insidious and odd. Much of the help provided to women in society is done through volunteer organizations and charities. These range from rape-relief shelters to business groups trying to get more women involved in politics. As charitable organizations they can obtain certain tax breaks. However, if they engage in "advocacy" work, these tax benefits are often taken away. In others words, charitable organizations can't pressure their elected government to make systemic change. In my opinion this is paramount to telling those in the trenches – those who understand the difficulties facing women – that they can only provide bandages when heart surgery is needed. They can provide immediate support to women who are suffering but can't speak to government about dealing with deeper causes and bigger solutions.

Although many of our laws discriminate against mothers in many ways, there are only a handful of legal academics who understand the laws and can write about them from a critical perspective. I saw a recent news article about a woman who demanded the removal of taxes on tampons since they were necessities. The government gave in – but it took 5 years of fighting. Funny how it finally passed just prior to an election!

Some governments understand how women struggle in society and within our current institutions and set up an office specifically to monitor and address this situation. In Canada, for example, there is a federal office called the "Status of Women Canada." Recently, however, funding was cut to this office. It is difficult to interpret this as anything but a reflection of our current government's low interest in tracking the status of women and creating programs to end discrimination and advance women in society.

Most people don't know where to even start when they see a law that is biased or unfair. However, by not participating in the legislative process we allow governments to maintain policies that hold women, families and children back. Indeed, it took a strong-willed group of women lawyers to create the Legal Education and Action Fund (LEAF). This organization is dedicated to only one thing: Challenging laws that discriminate against women. Sadly, these complex legal cases can take years to wind through the courts as they can be expensive and time consuming and don't normally generate a lot of media attention in the early stages.

Those governments that see children as important create laws and social programs to help them flourish. Those who do not value mothers do not introduce laws, policies or programs that support them. And because of this many of our current laws not only do not support women, but actually hold women back.

The Bottom Line. Many of our current laws, policies and programs hold women back. Indeed these hidden laws impact every one of us every day. The most obvious relate to economics such as funding for childcare and education. Other laws like corporate laws, charity laws, divorce laws and tax laws hold women back but because they are so complicated and difficult to change they rarely get challenged. Working in combination these laws and policies keep mothers trapped at home, excluded from the workplace and economically slipping behind. Worse still, women and particularly mothers are absent and rarely invited into the law-making process.

What To Do. We need to look closely at how our laws and policies impact women and we must challenge those that hold women back. At a minimum, mothers should demand publicly funded childcare. Mothers should seek compensation or income tax deductions for all expenses incurred in the course of raising children. As well, they should seek changes to corporate laws relating to taking time off for family obligations, flexible work and transparent hiring and promoting. This will enable mothers to have careers without having to sacrifice families. Most importantly we must teach women how to engage in the law-making process and work at making the process more accessible.

Chapter 13

Understand and Participate in Government

"Once we got out of the house, unlike our European sisters, we failed to make demands of our government for paid family leaves, workplace flexibility and quality child care. American feminist groups claim that child care was on their agenda from the start."
~ Madeline Kunin

I often tell my friends that if women knew how the government was truly behaving, they would revolt tomorrow. They would create an Occupy Women Movement. Not only do many laws discriminate against women, but every single day decisions are made by elected officials that prevent women from being equal or free. Yet we do not even see it. For this reason it is critical that every woman pay attention to how her elected government is spending her money and that she tell her elected officials how she thinks it could be better spent. To do this we need to understand how government works.

In a nutshell, we elect individual politicians and they meet together and make decisions on two things. They decide how much money to collect (through individual and corporate taxes) and they make decisions about how to spend the money. The way they spend the money must be done "for the public good." That's pretty much it.

As for collecting taxes, governments continually tinker with how much to tax citizens. They know if they go too far, taxpayers will revolt, but they need lots of money to run the country. From sales tax, gas tax, alcohol tax, property tax and corporate taxes, the goal is to collect enough money to ensure that the economy and our society flourish.

When it comes to spending our money, day in and day out our governments allocate money to the projects and programs they think are most important. Each of the various municipal, state, provincial and federal governments is continually figuring out how to spend dollars wisely. The sole aim is to spend money for "the public good."

Although this is very broad, at a minimum governments try to ensure that everyone has food, water and the necessities of life, for now and in the future. Our elected governments spend huge amounts of money on roads, bridges, police, prisons, hospitals and armies. When governments allocate funds to help people who are destitute, this is called social security. When they allocate funds to keep our population healthy, this is called the health care system. Their job is to look past the individual self-interests of citizens and seek goals that are for the long-term benefit of our whole society. That is why governments built railways and fund armies that may never go to war.

Although many governments suggest that our free market system is the main driver of our economy and society, this is not entirely true. Governments are major players and touch every single one of us every day through laws and institutions. So it's important to pay attention. Many grassroots organizations are dedicated to this type of work – the work of paying attention. One such organization is called Generation Squeeze. It looks at the way governments are helping and hindering the newest generation of parents, those who can barely own a home and raise a family.

Expanding on this topic is the book *The War Against Parents*, by Sylvia Ann Hewlett and Cornel West, which describes how government policy makes it so difficult to raise families. The authors recommend a "Parents Bill of Rights," including paid parenting leave, family friendly workplaces, a living wage, tax relief, help with housing, votes for children, extended school day, childcare, safe communities, among other ideas. Here are some very real policies that many groups have suggested that would advance women:

- $10-a-day childcare
- Child bonus checks
- Income splitting of husband and wife
- Maternity leave policies
- Corporate funded in-house day care
- Flex work and job sharing
- Insurance and benefits for mothers
- Programs to get women back into the workforce
- Alimony for divorced mothers

One of the best books on policies affecting mothers is *Leaving Women Behind* by Kimberley Strassel, Celeste Colgan and John Goodman from the National Center for Policy Analysis. It describes the ways American families have changed and how our laws have not kept in step. As a result the laws penalize parents for having children. Here are a few of the authors' suggestions for change (as edited by me):

- Change employee benefits so couples who both earn incomes do not both pay for health care and other employee benefits. They could receive income instead.
- Change employment laws so that those working less than full-time hours (i.e., 40 hours a week) have rights and give incentives to employers to provide flex and part-time work.
- Make sure parents who stay at home with children have adequate health and disability insurance.
- Adjust laws so health and retirement benefits are portable if we switch jobs.

This is why it's so important that women vote. The people we elect make thousands of decisions that can either harm or support mothers. I hate it when I hear that wives tend to vote for the same people that their husbands do. I wish it was simply a coincidence but I suspect it has more to do with wives being too busy to educate themselves on all the issues that impact their lives. This is unfortunate for two reasons. Husbands may not really know all the issues either and they may have very different interests than their wives.

Related to this is political action. Once women understand how the government works they can take action; there are many ways to do so. The most obvious is to try to change the law by partaking in the legislative process. This might involve asking for a commission to be appointed to look at the issue or recommending specific changes to statutes. Unfortunately changing the law can take many years, so another option is to become a person at the table.

This can be done by joining discussions that are happening on various topics or by getting elected and representing your electorate in advancing a cause. You could join an advocacy organization or work as a policy person in government. Easiest of all is simply speaking out publicly, whether to government, at parent meetings or around your kitchen table. If you are really keen you could start a movement and mobilize those concerned. At a minimum, mothers must vote for governments that are interested in creating laws and policies that advance women. As Judith Warner says, we need to challenge the stigma that suggests that, "It is not permissible to talk about policy or economics or culture – these words are somehow tacky..."

The Bottom Line. Government decisions impact mothers every single day yet mothers are notoriously absent around the tables of law-makers, decision-makers and government policy-makers. This is partly because our political system is not overly inviting and is frankly designed in a way that actively seems to keep mothers out. It is also because the average person may not know how government works or how to influence policy decisions. There are many ways, but the obvious ones are to engage in changing the law, become a person at the table by getting elected, work as a policy person in government, advocate or speak out to government or mobilize those concerned.

What To Do. The following are some specific activities to help change the laws and policies relating to mothers:

- Read the newspapers, subscribe to a newsfeed, read blogs, watch the news – in other words, start to search out news on policies that impact families.
- Join a political party and attend meetings in which they discuss policies.
- Become familiar with your politicians; visit their offices, watch their press conferences, tune in during election time.
- Attend rallies and demonstrations.
- Blog and write articles on topics that concern you.
- Write Opinion Editorials (Op-eds) in any big newspaper.
- Follow those journalists who reflect your ideas.
- Run for office.

Chapter 14

Encourage Mothers to Speak Up

"Patriarchy would seem to require, not only that women shall assume the major burden of pain and self-denial for the furtherance of the species, but that majority of the species – women – shall remain essentially unquestioning and unenlightened." ~ Adrienne Rich

"Being a Silent Woman is not about being quiet and reticent, it's about stifling our truth. Our real truth, ... [v]ery often silence becomes the female drug of choice." ~ Sue Monk Kidd

Have you ever noticed how mothers rarely complain? At least not publicly. Because things will not improve for mothers unless they speak up and out, it is important to both notice the barriers that silence women and also the supports women need to build their confidence and speak out without fear.

Over my many years of researching women in society I have noticed that there are three main reasons for women's silence: fear, lack of interest or energy and ignorance.

From a very early age we socialize girls to be silent. We expect them to be seen and not heard, as well as to be inclusive and agreeable. We thrust them into the role that they enjoy, which is relating to others, and then we crank up the heat. As social conveners we expect girls and women to not just be polite but to be excruciatingly nice, demanding that they somehow ensure that everyone gets along. We teach them that disagreements are distasteful and conflicts are terrifying and are something to be avoided. As a result, females learn in no uncertain terms that they should never speak out, but also that they should discourage others from speaking out, particularly women. Even though we may be fighting for something positive, we just don't want to do anything that might be messy. Like a revolt. We think that if we say anything about women's rights we will be seen as confrontational.

Women may not only fear conflict but may also fear any big displays of emotion. Recently a friend of mine was describing her family and told me that as she was growing up, she was sent to her room if she showed any display of sadness or frustration. As we continued to talk she also recalled that she was discouraged from laughing and shouting. Indeed, by the time we finished our conversation we came to the realization that her family was not unique. Parents stifle girls when they see their daughters acting in ways that don't seem "feminine."

As girls, this socialization is compounded by the pressure to be "seen and not heard:" to be quiet and polite and, in some cases, invisible. We are urged to be nice to everyone and to not say anything that might disrupt a relationship. Some girls learn that lying is appropriate, since telling the truth might be painful to someone. This conditioning is reinforced throughout our lives and is the main reason why women today do not speak out. They may speak out for others but they rarely speak out against personal injustices, since this would be considered selfish and unfeminine.

In playing this role, women work hard at staying upbeat. So, for example, instead of agreeing that mothers carry a heavy burden, they often neutralize or change a topic since it causes discomfort. Women are masters at sidestepping arguments and do almost anything they can to avoid hurting others' feelings.

One way this can be manifested is through displaying a lack of interest. When I am speaking out about my research on women's slow advancement, I often hear things like, "Wow, your book sounds very interesting, how are your girls doing?" Sometimes friends try to convince me that things aren't that bad, tilting their heads slightly, saying something like, "What on earth could you write about? All the women I know are powerful." But to complain is completely out of the question. No matter how bad things get, mothers are expected to suck it up. Indeed I often hear mothers saying the exact same things to their children! This phrase clearly reflects our belief that we are powerless or have no ability to change things, so it makes practical sense to simply accept things as they are. This feeling of powerlessness, however, can lead to depression, self-hatred and deep-seated resentment.

If a mother does complain, it is also highly likely that her comments will be perceived as criticism of her children. Since we are told that mothers are mostly to blame for a child's problematic behavior, they risk making themselves look bad or incompetent by saying anything. Sometimes mothers' complaints are even seen as suggesting that the mother does not love her children, which is doubly taboo.

Although women do on occasion speak up, they tend to do it on behalf of others, and not themselves. Many enjoy speaking out for those weaker than themselves, such as young girls, but have learned that it is inappropriate, risky and selfish to try to gain something for themselves. Often underlying this cocktail of fears is the deeper fear of being rejected or excluded. As girls we learned that if we want to be included we must treat each other well. We must be soft spoken and inclusive. We must not speak aggressively or rock the boat in any way. I call this the "pacification of females." It's a big problem.

As authors Susan Douglas and Meredith Michaels write in their book, *The Mommy Myth*, we are taught that if we want to be the perfect mother then we should not be entertaining, "thoughts about the meaning of life, world peace, finding a cure for polio, let alone feelings of resentment, anxiety, depression, boredom, envy, frustration, or anger at a husband who might, on occasion, spend half his salary on beers for the guys and a friend named 'Lola'."

Indeed, even I often stay silent, unless I am in the company of supportive women. I rarely mention the word patriarchy or power because these words not only kill conversation but cause such discomfort in some women that they will avoid future contact with me. Judith Warner suggests, however, that by silencing ourselves we force ourselves to remove it from our minds completely, severing our thoughts as well as our ability to feel. She says, "And so women don't. Think about it. Or fight. Or even feel."

In fact, research shows that when we do not speak up, we cause ourselves even bigger problems. According to Jeanne Elium and Don Elium, "[Women] give themselves away. To avoid causing pain or inconvenience to others, they swallow their own needs and feelings. This loss of voice turns into resentment, eating disorders, rage, depression, low self-esteem, dependency and sexual dysfunction. They learn to be manipulative, indirect and passive to get what they need." However, the cost of not expressing emotions, particularly anger, are very high. By denying and not expressing emotions, we suffer deep internal conflicts. When we do not express anger directly, it shows up in our lives in distorted ways. Although women might tell others that everything is okay, they will secretly talk with friends about lack of sex or their husbands' inability to communicate or contribute to the family. They may accuse their husbands and all men of being selfish, stupid and inconsiderate or blame them for making them slaves to their homes.

Naomi Wolf, in her book *Misconceptions,* suggests that mothers nurse a "quite stubborn knot of resentment" that looks like "passive aggression" and that they may withhold sex as a way of evening the score. However, most eventually give up because, "what, after all was the point of being mad all the time?"

One way the media has silenced mothers is by pitting them against one another and calling it the "Mommy Wars." As Warner writes, the Mommy Wars are premised on the false notion that some mothers choose the "selfish," modern track of ambition and others choose the "selfless," natural track of the stay-at-home mom, and that the two sides don't see eye to eye. This myth keeps the spotlight on women, suggesting that the problem is not societal expectations, but rather a moral or religious difference. As research shows, however, often motherhood is driven more by practical necessity under pressure than a personal philosophy.

Leslie Bennetts suggests that arguing in this way is a complete waste of valuable time and energy since the entire debate over the Mommy Wars misses the real point. Motherhood is ultimately an economic decision, not a value difference, as suggested here:

> Imagine how productive it would be if we stopped obsessing on the morality of staying at home versus working and focused instead on the material conditions that stress all mothers to the point where they founder and drown in The Mess. First of all, we would find working mothers and stay-at-home moms' interests, ambitions, goals, and needs were strongly aligned. And then, by focusing on the facts of their lives, we would be able to start to define some national priorities for policy that would actually help ease families' lives.

Another powerful tool that silences women is guilt. Don't you think it's odd that every mother that I know feels horribly guilty? No matter what choice they have made, whether to stay at home, to work for pay or to do a combination of the two, they stress about it. And to make things worse, this guilt drives women to rationalize their choices and convince themselves not only that this is the right way to do it, but also that the other way is wrong.

As for ignorance as a barrier to women speaking out, I wrote this book because of the lack of available information on the topic of motherhood. Not only are there very few books, most are written by academics and don't often provide solutions. I am never surprised when women have no idea about the institution of motherhood. This information is extraordinarily difficult to find. This ignorance is reinforced by the media who continually tell women that motherhood is blissful and that balance is achieved through small steps and a bit of effort. The media takes society's definition of the perfect, happy and loving mother then broadcasts it everywhere. From television sitcoms and advertising to novels and magazines, we are never told that the role of motherhood is oppressive. The underlying message is that if motherhood is problematic, then it's our own fault.

Think about it, what more could you ask for than a never complaining, always conciliatory wife and mother who cheerfully helps around the house? This perfect mother does not want to work outside the home and because she possesses a maternal instinct, loves nurturing all children. She loves decorating and gardening and polishing silver and entertaining her husband's boss. She is marginally interested in current affairs especially new gadgets to make all her chores a bit easier.

But there is another truth no one wants women to know. It is this: We all benefit in some way when mothers stick with the status quo and do not rock the boat. Husbands benefit when women do the housework for free, the children love her being there and sacrificing her career for them, the government is thrilled not to have to pay her or millions of other mothers for childcare. Moreover our whole society loves the fact that mothers will raise our next generation and sacrifice themselves doing so. Who else but mothers will complain about the state of motherhood? No one else feels the pain.

The Bottom Line. When it comes to talking about women's rights, women tend to stay silent. This is partly due to fear but also because of ignorance and lack of interest or energy. It's no wonder mothers are deeply afraid. We have been told since childhood that we must be silent and nice. We are condemned if we complain, we are told to suck it up and stop being so selfish and we gain an aversion to conflict. We are kept in the dark about the shadow side of motherhood because information is hard to find and the media convinces us that motherhood is blissful. Even if we did have the courage, there is little time or energy left in our crazy busy lives to challenge the trap of motherhood.

What To Do. We must identify the specific tools used to silence women and stop blaming women for not speaking up. We must stop demanding that all women be nice all the time. We must recognize the constant social conditioning and the very real risks women face when they tell the truth to power. We must support women in any way possible and provide safe places for them to voice concerns without fear of attack or negative consequences. We must speak out against those who wish to pacify us and must never shame a woman or criticize her for simply stating her truth. Most importantly, we must free women from their heavy burdens of life so they have a bit more time to consider these matters and speak out. It would be fantastic to have thousands of small groups of women gathering in mutual support and as communities for change.

Chapter 15

Educate Your Daughters about Marriage

> "There is no way that motherhood will be anything other than oppressive if the power relationships a mother has with husband, parents, doctors, repair people, and school personnel are not equalized. For children learn to treat their mother exactly as they observe others treat her. Just as children learn to treat with great respect people who receive respect from others, children learn to demean and put down those who are treated with disrespect by others." ~ Selma Greenberg

We mothers rarely teach our daughters about the world of men and women in marriage. We barely know about it ourselves and we hardly know about the legalities of marriage until we are in trouble in our relationships. However, the most important legal contract your daughter may enter into is a contract of marriage.

Even though about 90% of girls will get married, we don't talk about it in the high school curriculum or in any university or college courses, except perhaps in a gender studies program. Nor do most parents know enough about the institution of motherhood to be able to teach their own daughters. It's not their fault, it's invisible.

Unwittingly our daughters, like us, are impacted by laws, institutions and rules that they may not even know exist. On her wedding day, a bride enters into a written contract of marriage. In doing so she may inadvertently become dependent on her husband and as a result, perhaps without even realizing it, lose her sense of equality and power. And things can go downhill from there, unless she has prepared herself and knows what is likely to happen during her marriage and the risks she is taking.

It is up to parents to tell their daughters about the hurdles and challenges they will face when they become wives and mothers. This dialogue should happen; daughters need to know about any potential barriers and how they are unique to being female in our society. Although I recommend that all girls read this book, if this is not possible here are the top things that I told my daughters about life after marriage to a man:

- You will likely earn less than your husband, even if you are in a similar job.
- You will likely have fewer advancement opportunities than your husband.
- You will likely do more than 70% of the household chores even if you have a paying job.
- You will likely do more than 80% of raising your children.
- You will likely carry the responsibility of hiring and managing childcare if you need it.
- If you divorce, you will likely be in a worse financial situation than your husband.
- If you take off time to raise kids you will find it very difficult to get back into a high paying job.
- If you divorce and keep the kids you will find it difficult to find high paying, flexible work.
- If you give up your career you will lose not just money, but your pension and insurance.

- If you divorce after raising kids your ex-husband will not likely want to give you any money to compensate you for giving up your career to raise your kids.

- If you depend entirely on your husband for money it is likely you will suffer a loss of self-worth and low self-esteem and will often feel powerless in your relationship with your husband.

This is not speculation. This is what happens in our current society. If your daughters do not want this to happen, they will need to work very hard to work around it because many of our institutions are so inflexible that living a balanced life is very difficult.

One of my pet peeves is the use of the title "Mrs." and the fact that many women change their names to their husbands' last name when they marry. Many people do not recall that women used to be thought of as their husbands' property. When they got married they gave up their names to reflect ownership. Although modern women are no longer considered possessions, most still take their husbands' names. Some argue that it is for the benefit of the children, so they have the same surname, however, there is always the option of taking the woman's name instead of the man's. There are many options. I've heard of couples using the mother's last name for two of their girls, and the father's last name for the other two. It works for them, but as Catherine Dee writes, "Some brides are aware that the tradition is sexist, but for various and totally valid reasons – such as not wanting to burden their children with long hyphenated last names – they go along with the custom."

As Susan Douglas and Meredith Michaels say, "Why should women have to take their husbands' last names when they get married, thereby symbolically eradicating their previous identity?"

Related to abandoning your own surname on marriage and the use of "Mrs." is the use of the husband's first name as well. As all women know, they can keep their first name or abandon it too, choosing Mrs. Howard Smith rather than Mrs. Jeannette Smith. Men usually only have one way of being addressed: "Mr." But women have three ways in which they can be described in their title, all indicating their marital status: single (Miss), married (Mrs.) and neutral (Ms.). Historically it was critical for a woman to get married to survive. Since she was not allowed to have money or a job, it was important to announce her single-ness to attract a suitor. The labels Miss and Mrs. actually mean "mistress of, or possession of a man," since women who were either daughters or wives were seen as a benefit to men and conferred a slightly higher status. It also meant, however, that you belonged to and were supported by a man.

Unfortunately, however, marital status is still used to discriminate against women. Many married women are treated unfairly when applying for jobs or when being promoted, on the assumption that a wife does not need money as much as a husband does. To allow women to keep their marital status private and avoid discrimination, the feminist movement (through Gloria Steinem) introduced the term "Ms." into our lexicon. In effect, it gives women the same privacy and freedom from possible bias that men have always had. I feel that the time is ripe to end the use of the term "Mrs." Every time you fill out a form and it asks you to check one of three boxes (Miss, Mrs. or Ms.), call up the company and ask them to change their policy so that only Ms. is an option. Never allow anyone to call you Mrs. again! Tell them you have decided to enter the 21st century and want to gain the same neutral designation men have always enjoyed.

The Bottom Line. Right now, our daughters do not learn about marriage or the institution of motherhood at school or in college. Without this understanding they tend to fall unwittingly into marriage and face all sorts of barriers and expectations that hold them back and limit their choices. Few know that it is likely their husbands will earn more than they will or that they will face brutal discrimination as a mother and as a female worker. They don't know they will likely end up doing most of the childcare and housework even if they have a full-time job.

What To Do. We as parents have a responsibility to daughters to tell them about what happens to them when they decide to marry and have children. It is grossly unfair to allow them to stumble into this system and simply accept unfairness and inequality. Make dinner table discussions count. Be a role model. Give them one or many of the books listed in this book's suggested reading list. Better yet, hand them this book. As they enter into the big life decisions, its best if they have their eyes open.

Conclusion

"In my [ideal] world the question to the working mothers would not be, 'How are "you" going to find childcare for "your" children while you work?' The world I would give my daughter would ask, 'How can we "together" find solutions to enable women the freedom to work while raising healthy children, because they are our collective future?'" ~ Jeanne Elium and Don Elium

Motherhood Is Madness shows that today's mothers are overworked and undervalued. They are depressed and exhausted, not because of some genetic predisposition but rather because of the institution of motherhood – or what some call "momism" or "the sticky floor" – a system that evolved over hundreds of years, but currently consists of many barriers and biases that hold mothers back.

This system was labelled 20 years ago as the institution of motherhood by Adrienne Rich in her best-selling book, *Of Woman Born* and in several more recent books, such as *The Mommy Myth* by Susan Douglas and Meredith Michaels.

This institution that sets out the laws and rules by which mothers and their families function is no longer a good fit with the realities of today's society. It not only holds women back, but harms spouses, children and whole families.

At its core is the expectation that mothers will be intensive mothers, caring for children and meeting all of their needs 24/7. In this model mothers are expected to not only sacrifice themselves and their careers to their children, but must do this to a level of near perfection without much help from husbands or the public at large. If mothers wish to have a career as well as a family it is made so difficult and financially unviable that they either quit their jobs or stretch themselves painfully thin.

This institution goes unchallenged because it is largely invisible; it is accepted as the status quo. As well, mothers are discouraged from complaining and are persuaded by rhetoric that this type of motherhood is not only natural but blissful.

For almost 100 years, suffragists and feminists fought hard against this institution as well as sexist and discriminatory laws and corporate policies. But while they were focusing on political power, such as the right to vote, and economic power, such as the right to work and own property, they seemed to overlook the home front – the ultimate barrier. Feminism has more work to do, not only for mothers but in addressing the remaining deep-rooted cultural beliefs holding women back. These underlie the legal, policy and institutional barriers of today. As long as these barriers exist, women cannot contribute fully in the world in a free and robust way.

Luckily, at this point in history, particularly with Internet access, many women are waking up. Some are choosing to be childfree while others are demanding changes to taxes, policies and programs that would lift some of the burdens they face. Others are realizing that they are not alone and with the recent acceptance (and even popularity) of the word "feminism," women are realizing they can tell the truth about their lives.

So what is the solution? Here are some easy steps:

Step 1. We must talk about motherhood as an institution and acknowledge mothers' reality. We must notice how women struggle and understand the link between "women's problems" (such as depression and stress) and the whole institution. We must refrain from blaming women for "getting into this mess" and understand how we created and maintain it.

Step 2. We must look at the various parts of this institution and how they work together to keep women down. This includes the 24/7 demands of both home and work, the costs attached to raising children and domestic and extended family burdens. We must look at all factors that push women out of workplaces and keep them out, even after children have grown. We must notice the factors that force women to make impossible choices. We must also be careful not to make judgments about the choices women make. We must refrain from telling women that they must either stay at home or go to work and instead urge them to be true to themselves.

Step 3. We must take action. Talking is not enough. We must stop asking women to do all the child rearing and take on all the social, emotional and domestic responsibilities, particularly without reward or recognition. It's not fair to expect them to be martyrs to our next generation. We must work, men and women together, as partners to build a new model of motherhood based on principles of equality. We must commit to helping mothers be happy and fulfilled. As Judith Warner says, "I do not think that women can be happy in our current culture of motherhood. It is just too psychologically damaging."

After all is said and done, perhaps the most important thing we can do as individuals is believe that all this thinking about empowering mothers is possible. A first step is to create a vision of what is ideal. Here are some of the ideas from the book, *If Women Ruled the World*, edited by Sheila Ellison and Marie Wilson:

- Women's work would not be defined as housework.
- Stay-at-home fathers would be commonplace.
- Equal parenting would be the norm instead of the exception.
- Stay-at-home parenting would be counted as paid work (with retirement benefits).
- The work versus family trade off wouldn't exist.

- Being happy would be a career goal.
- Family court orders would be enforced.
- We would value the health of our children more than big business.
- Baby girls would always be cause to celebrate!

Where to now?

Until I wrote this book, I thought that I was all alone. I felt completely out of balance and often felt inadequate as both a mother, wife and a lawyer – and too ashamed to tell anyone about it. Now I know that millions of mothers feel just like me and I am pleased to say: You are not going crazy and neither am I. There is nothing wrong with you but there is something very wrong with the way we treat mothers.

If you really want to empower mothers the first step is easy. Simply share what you have learned in this book. Give this book to a mother. Buy it for a friend or her daughter. Share the 15 strategies at the end of this book (*Motherhood – A Manifesto to Empower Mothers*). Copy the list and distribute it to your friends and neighbors. Share it on social media (contact the author for an electronic version). Talk to other mothers. Simply have conversations. That's how it all begins and you might be amazed at what might emerge.

After all: If not now, when? If not you, then who?

Motherhood – A Manifesto to Empower Mothers

15 Strategies

1. Admit that Motherhood Is Madness
2. Stop Asking Mothers to Choose Career or Family
3. Don't Expect Women to Be Unpaid Servants
4. Never Expect Mothers to be Martyrs to Kids
5. Recognize the Importance of Mothering
6. Make Childcare Available, Affordable and Acceptable
7. Question the 24/7 Work Culture and the Mommy Penalty
8. Ensure Mothers are Financially Independent
9. Adopt a Partnership Model of the Family
10. Value Mothers, Children and Families
11. Compensate and Invest in Mothers
12. Challenge Laws that Hold Women Back
13. Understand and Participate in Government
14. Encourage Mothers to Speak Up
15. Educate Your Daughters About Marriage

Selected Bibliography

Alcorn, Katrina. *Maxed Out: American Moms on the Brink*. Seal Press, 2013.

Badinter, Elisabeth. *The Conflict: How Modern Motherhood Undermines the Status of Women*. Metropolitan Books, 2012.

Bennetts, Lesie. *The Feminine Mistake: Are We Giving Up Too Much?* Hyperion, 2007.

Collins, Gale. *When Everything Changed: The Amazing Journey of American Women from 1960 to the Present.* Little, Brown & Co., 2009.

Crittenden, Ann. *The Price of Motherhood: Why the Most Important Job in the World is Still the Least Valued.* Picador, 2010.

Crittenden, Daniele. *What Our Mothers Didn't Tell Us: Why Happiness Eludes the Modern Woman.* Simon & Shuster, 2000.

De Beauvoir, Simone. *The Second Sex.* Knopf, 1953.

Dee, Catherine. *A Girls' Guide to Life: Take Charge of Your Personal Life, Your School Time, Your Social Scene, and Much More!* Little Brown, 2005.

Douglas, Susan J. and Meredith W. Michaels. *The Mommy Myth: The Idealization of Motherhood and How It Has Undermined All Women.* Free Press, 2004.

Edelman, Hope. "The Myth of Co-Parenting: How It Was Supposed to Be. How It Was" in Cathi Hanauer (ed.). *The Bitch in the House: 26*

Women Tell the Truth About Sex, Solitude, Work, Motherhood and Marriage. Perennial, 2003.

Eisler, Riane. *The Chalice and the Blade: Our History, Our Future.* Harper San Francisco, 1988.

——. *The Power of Partnership: Seven Relationships that Will Change Your Life.* New World Library, 2002.

——. *The Real Wealth of Nations: Creating a Caring Economics.* Berrett-Koehler, 2007.

Elium, Jeanne and Don Elium. *Raising a Daughter: Parents and the Awakening of a Healthy Woman*. Celestial Arts, 2003.

Ellison, Sheila (ed.) and Marie Wilson. *If Women Ruled the World: How to Create the World We Want to Live In.* New World Library, 2004.

Engberg, Karen. *It's Not the Glass Ceiling: It's the Sticky Floor. And Other Things Our Daughters Should Know about Marriage, Work, and Motherhood.* Prometheus, 1999.

Evans, Gail. *She Wins, You Win: The Most Important Rule Every Business Woman Needs to Know.* Gotham, 2003.

Fisher, Helen. *The First Sex: The Natural Talents of Women and How They Are Changing the World.* Random House, 2000.

Fitzgerald, Maureen. *Lean Out: How to Dismantle the Corporate Barriers that Hold Women Back*. CenterPoint Media, 2016.

——. *Occupy Women: A Manifesto for Positive Change in a World Run by Men*. CenterPoint Media, 2016.

——. *Wake Up Sleeping Beauty: Protect your Daughter from Sexism, Stereotypes and Sexualisation.* CenterPoint Media, 2016.

Friedan, Betty. *The Feminine Mystique.* Norton, 1963.

Gilligan, Carol. *In a Different Voice: Psychological Theory and Women's Development*. Harvard University Press, 1982.

Greenberg, Selma. *Right from the Start. A Guide to Non-sexist Child Rearing.* Houghton Mifflin, 1979.

Hanauer, Cathi (ed.). *The Bitch in the House: 26 Women Tell the Truth About Sex, Solitude, Work, Motherhood and Marriage.* Perennial, 2003.

Hewlett, Sylvia Ann. *Off Ramps and On Ramps: Keeping Talented Women on the Road to Success.* Harvard Business Review Press, 2007.

—— and Cornel West. *The War Against Parents: What We Can Do for America's Beleaguered Moms and Dads*. Houghton Mifflin, 1998.

Hochschild, Arlie R. and Anne Machung. *The Second Shift*. Penguin, 2003.

Kidd, Sue Monk. *Dance of the Dissident Daughter: A Women's Journey from Christian Tradition to the Sacred Feminine.* Harper, 1996.

Kunin, Madeline. *The New Feminist Agenda: Defining the Next Revolution for Women, Work, and Family.* Chelsea Green Publishing, 2012.

Lerner, Sharon. *The War on Moms: On Life in a Family Unfriendly Nation*. John Wiley, 2010.

Lewis, Susan. *Reinventing Ourselves after Motherhood: How Former Career Women Refocus their Personal and Professional Lives After the Birth of a Child*. Contemporary Books, 1999.

Maier, Corinne. *No Kids! 40 Good Reasons Not to Have Children.* McClelland & Stewart, 2009.

McKinnon, Catherine. *Feminism Unmodified: Discourses on Life and Law.* Harvard University Press, 1988.

Meers, Sharon and Joanna Strober. *Getting to 50/50: How Working Parents Can Have it All.* Viva Editions, 2013.

Miles, Rosalind. *Who Cooked the Last Super: The Women's History of the World*. Broadway Books, 2001.

Miller, Jean Baker and Irene Stiver. *The Healing Connection: How Women Form Relationships in Therapy and Life*. Beacon Press, 1998.

Moen, Phyllis and Patricia Roehling. *The Career Mystique: Cracks in the American Dream.* Rowman and Littlefield, 2004.

Murdock, Maureen. *The Heroine's Journey*. Shambhala, 1990.

O'Reilly, Andrea (ed.). *Mother Outlaws: Theories and Practices of Empowered Mothering.* Women's Press, 2004.

Rice, Curt. "The Motherhood Penalty: It's not Children that Slow Mothers Down." December 8, 2011, accessed August 3, 2015 at curt-rice.com/2011/12/08/the-motherhood-penalty-its-not-children-that-slow-mothers-down/.

Rich, Adrienne. *Of Woman Born: Motherhood as Experience and Institution.* W.W. Norton, 1976.

Roberts, Anita. *Safe Teen: Powerful Alternatives to Violence.* Polestar Books, 2001.

Sandberg, Sheryl. *Lean In: Women, Work and the Will to Lead.* Knopf, 2013.

Schaef, Anne Wilson. *Meditations for Women Who Do Too Much.* HarperCollins, 1990.

——. *Women's Reality: An Emerging Female System in a White Male Society*. Harper & Row, 1985.

Schafer, Alyson. *Breaking the Good Mom Myth.* Collins Canada, 2014.

Seeley, Meagan. *Fight Like a Girl. How to Be a Fearless Feminist.* New York University Press, 2007.

Silverstein, Shel. *The Giving Tree*. Harper & Row, 1964.

Solovic, Susan. *The Girls' Guide to Power and Success.* Amacom, 2001.

Stone, Pamela. "Fast-Track Women and the 'Choice' to Stay Home." *The Annals of the American Academy of Political and Social Science*, November 2004.

Stone, Sidra. *The Shadow King: The Invisible Force that Holds Women Back*. iUniverse, 1997.

Strassel, Kimberley, Celeste Colgan and John Goodman. *Leaving Women Behind: Modern Families, Outdated Laws.* Rowman & Littlefield, 2007.

Valenti, Jessica. *He's a Stud, She's a Slut and 49 Other Double Standards Every Woman Should Know*. Seal Press, 2008.

——. *Full Frontal Feminism: A Young Woman's Guide to Why Feminism Matters.* Seal Press, 2008.

Warner, Judith. *Perfect Madness: Motherhood in the Age of Anxiety.* Riverhead, 2005.

Williams, Joan C. and Rachel Dempsey. *What Women Want at Work: Four Patterns Working Women Need to Know.* New York University Press, 2014.

WIlliamson, Marianne. *A Woman's Worth.* Ballantine, 1994.

Wilson, H. W. *Revisiting Gender: The Reference Shelf*. Grey House Publishing, 2014.

Wolf, Naomi. *The Beauty Myth: How Images of Beauty are Used Against Women*. Doubleday, 1991.

——. *Misconceptions: Truth, Lies and the Unexpected on the Journey to Motherhood.* Anchor, 2003.

About the Author

Maureen F. Fitzgerald, PhD, JD, LLM, BComm is a recovering lawyer, author and change agent. She practiced law for over 20 years and is the founder of CenterPoint Media, a multimedia publisher of books that advance thinking.

In her former life, Maureen was a labor lawyer, a policy lawyer and a mediator. She was also a professor of law at two universities and has written twelve books and many articles – both academic and practical. She has a business degree, two law degrees, a masters' degree in law from the London School of Economics and a doctorate degree in philosophy.

Always a leader of both people and ideas, Maureen speaks across North America about social justice, equality and mindfulness. Her motto is: *Sharing the right ideas at the right time can change the world.*

Maureen is the author of the following books:

- ***Lean Out***: *How to Dismantle the Corporate Barriers that Hold Women Back.*
- ***Motherhood is Madness***: *How to Break the Chains that Prevent Mothers from Being Truly Happy.*
- ***Occupy Women***: *A Manifesto for Positive Change in a World Run by Men.*
- ***A Woman's Circle:*** *Create a Peer Mentoring Group for Advice, Networking, Support and Connection.*

- ***Invite the Bully to Tea:*** *End Harassment, Bullying and Dysfunction Forever with a Simple yet Radical New Approach.*
- ***If Not Now, When?*** *Create a Life and Career of Purpose with a Powerful Vision, a Mission Statement and Measurable Goals.*
- ***Mindfulness Made Easy:*** *50 Simple Practices to Reduce Stress, Create Calm and Live in the Moment – At Home, Work and School.*
- ***Hiring, Managing and Keeping the Best:*** *The Complete Canadian Guide for Employers,* with Monica Beauregard.
- ***So You Think You Need a Lawyer:*** *How to Screen, Hire, Manage or Fire a Lawyer.*
- ***Legal Problem Solving:*** *Reasoning, Research and Writing (7ed).* Lexis/Nexis.
- ***Wake up Sleeping Beauty****: Protect Your Daughter from Sexism, Stereotypes and Sexualization [2016].*
- ***Mean Girls Aren't Mean****: Stand up to Cliques, Bullies, Peer Pressure and Popularity and Empower Girls in a Radical New Way [2016].*
- ***Gritty Is the New Pretty:*** *Raise Confident, Courageous and Resilient Girls in a Man's World [2016].*

You can find her at www.MaureenFitzgerald.com.

Books in This Series

Made in the USA
Charleston, SC
20 March 2016